Leading Apple
with Steve Jobs

Leading Apple with Steve Jobs

Management Lessons *from a* Controversial Genius

JAY ELLIOT

WILEY

John Wiley & Sons, Inc.

For my wife, Liliana, and my sons, Jay-Alexander, Federico, and Scott, for their tolerance of the time I spent on this book.

And in memory of Dr. Arynne Simon, the best coach I ever had.

Contents

Preface
Why I Wrote This Book

Like many others, I remember exactly what I was doing when I heard the news of Steve Jobs' passing. A friend of mine called on my cell phone as I was driving my 15-year-old son home from high school. He said, "Did you hear the news? Steve just died."

Immediately afterward, my phone rang again. This time it was a San Francisco radio station, wanting to interview me. I did the interview, but could hardly make it through. I was breaking up. After the call, I started sobbing and had to pull over to let my son drive. I hadn't cried since my mother died.

I started thinking about first meeting Steve, this hippie-like guy who struck up a conversation with me in a restaurant and a few minutes later wanted me to be his vice president of human resources at Apple and, at the same time, a member of the original Mac development team. I remembered being almost overwhelmed trying to keep up with Steve while helping him run Apple. Observing Steve close up changed my entire outlook on how to run a business and how to energize people to their highest level of creativity.

In my previous book, *The Steve Jobs Way*, I outlined the powerful leadership skills Steve had and developed along the way at Apple, NeXT, Pixar, and back at Apple, and, just as important, his ability to bounce back from the major failures. That book, published in the United States and in 27 foreign countries, led to hundreds of responses and inquiries from around the world for more information. Those requests led to the decision to write this book, focused on the how-to management lessons drawn from my observations of Steve Jobs' day-by-day leadership. I want to share my experience of Steve's basic strategies for leading his teams, and the things that made them so incredibly *innovative*. Shortly after my first book was published, Walter Isaacson's biography of Steve appeared. Though it was widely acclaimed and authorized by Steve, I found it unfairly negative and critical of him—and it misreported many events that I witnessed firsthand. I wasn't the only person who had this reaction. Bill Campbell, a former Apple vice president, longtime board member, and personal friend of Steve's, had harsh words for what he referred to as "that damn book." He criticized it for focusing far too much on the negative aspects of how Steve dealt with people. Steve has been widely accused of being insufferable while also acknowledged as a brilliant and motivational leader. Though of course he had flaws, Isaacson's Steve is not the Steve I knew.

It's true that one of my roles at Apple was to be the "adult" in the room and manage the fallout from the occasional mess Steve would create. Yet, on the whole, I think most people who worked for him, including me, would say they did the best work of their lives for him and don't regret the experience a bit. Not only that, but I've used the leadership lessons I learned from Steve throughout my career. The purpose of this book is to help you do the same.

There are two other important ways that this book is different from almost all the other Steve Jobs/Apple books out there. I tell a lot of stories about watching Steve in action at Apple, not as a journalist relying on the reports and opinions of others, but from the perspective of being there. This is a book about leadership, management, and innovation based on my personal experience as VP of human resources and then as senior VP of Apple. None of the other books I've read about Steve and Apple were written by people who were actually there, working side-by-side with him and helping him formulate his tactics for organizing teams and inspiring people to become even more creative and innovative.

When I worked at Apple, Steve was still in his 20s, and I was hired in part because Steve wanted a graybeard around. Because of my age and experience, and because of the knowledge from my years in management at IBM and Intel, I was the only person over 40 whose business opinions and advice he really trusted on a daily basis. He looked to me as both a mentor and as a guide. And yet, despite the fact that I was older and much more experienced in business, I found it incredibly inspiring to work with him. We were both motivated not by the money but by the goal of changing the world.

In these pages you will find practical examples that show how Steve's leadership principles can be used in the everyday worlds of business, of product development, and of recruiting and managing people. I've also added a special emphasis on his techniques for inspiring innovation.

Even though it's true Steve was a unique, charismatic leader and that he had flaws, there is a great deal that the average manager or leader can learn from his style and approach to motivating people, pursuing excellence, and assembling and leading innovative teams. I hope this book will help you inspire your people to do the best work of their lives.

Chronology

This book is organized around key management and leadership lessons I learned from Steve at Apple, not chronological events. The following may be helpful to return to later in the book, to clarify the context of a story or event.

1976   Steve Jobs and Steve Wozniak form Apple Computer, Inc.

1981   Steve Jobs takes over the Macintosh development team

1983   Steve convinces John Sculley, vice president of soft-drink company PepsiCo, to become CEO of Apple

1983   Macintosh goes on sale; with the mouse and a graphical user interface, it is the first easy-to-use personal computer

1985   Sculley and the board remove Steve from head of the Macintosh team; Steve leaves the company

1985   Steve starts NeXT, a competing personal computer company

1993   Sculley leaves Apple

1996   Apple acquires NeXT, bringing Steve back into Apple

1997   Steve becomes interim CEO of Apple

2000   Steve becomes full-fledged CEO

2000   Apple opens first retail store

2001   Steve introduces the iPod, the first in what will become a series of society-changing, noncomputer products

1

A Ding in the Universe

Everything Starts with an Inspiring Vision

I have looked in the mirror every morning and asked myself: "If today were the last day of my life, would I want to do what I am about to do today?" And whenever the answer has been "No" for too many days in a row, I know I need to change something.

—Steve Jobs

If Steve Jobs had been invited to speak to a class of business school students in the days of the first Apple computer and had been able to describe the management style he would eventually invent for Apple Computer, Inc., you can be pretty sure the professor would have thrown him out on his ear and told the students not to pay attention to anything he said. Steve's management style simply violated just about every rule that company men have lived by since the beginning of the Industrial Revolution.

And yet despite this and despite his flaws and the fact that he could be harshly critical and demanding, Steve's approach didn't just work, it made possible the flow of innovative products that have changed the way we live. In the process, Steve's approach has made Apple arguably the most successful company in the history of business.

1

Was this kind of leadership possible only because of Steve's particular, peculiar charismatic personality? I wrote this book because I don't think that's true.

Creating products so great that they can change society doesn't start with product development; it starts with a vision. Steve used to say that communicating your vision to your people is as important as creating a new product. His vision for how computers should interact with people is what made the original Macintosh so special and what motivated the development team to do the best work of their lives to create it. Steve's vision for how technology in general could be made friendly, human, and appealing eventually lead to the series of products so special that they eventually made Apple the most valuable company in the world.

Many articles and books have been written on the techniques and tactics Steve used as a manager of people. That has been fine as far as they go. But the striking thing is what few people recognize: that Steve, almost from the very beginning, understood and lived by the qualities of true leadership, not textbook leadership.

Rating Steve as a Leader

In light of the widespread criticism of Steve's management style, it's worth asking how the people who worked at Apple rated him as a leader and a boss. We have part of the answer, and a comparison to other leaders, thanks to a website called Glassdoor, where employees post their comments, rankings, and criticisms about the company they work for. Apple's employees have consistently ranked it as one of the best places to work in America; the current ranking as I write this is number 10, out of the thousands of companies the website ranks. The negative comments posted on Glassdoor tend to come not from the Apple troops in Cupertino but from people who work in the retail stores, where the tasks tend to be highly repetitive and the chances for promotion few.

It's interesting to note that Tim Cook, the CEO whom Steve Jobs tapped as his successor, while lacking Steve's magic and charisma, still receives a ranking from employees almost identical to Steve's, a near-perfect 96 versus Steve's 97. For comparison, the CEO of Google, Eric Schmidt, scored 92, while the former CEO of Hewlett-Packard, Meg Whitman, limped along with a pallid 76.

Much of this isn't surprising, but what struck me most about the CEO numbers was this: Steve Jobs was the only person on the list who did not have academic credentials.

The numbers tell us that Steve's leadership is now part of the culture. I will always believe that criticisms of his leadership style may not be based on complaints from within the Apple culture but grumblings that reporters and journalists built up to make their stories jucier. I was recently in an Apple store, and the employees recognized me as the author of *The Steve Jobs Way*. Two of the staff told me they thought the Isaacson authorized biography of Steve portrayed him in much too negative a light, while mine, they felt, much more closely captured their experience of him. I was pleased not just by the compliment but by the affirmation that Apple employees, even those who had perhaps felt his wrath, couldn't help but feel a warm appreciation for him. Steve Wozniak, Apple's cofounder with Steve, went so far as to say that Steve "is probably going to be remembered for the next hundred years as the best business leader of our time."

Soon after I started working at Apple as the vice president of human resources (and also as a member of the original Mac development team), Steve and I began talking about ways to get the whole team on the same page, and he decided to have an off-site meeting. I drew up a list of suggestions, and he settled on the Pajaro Dunes Resort on the Pacific Ocean in Northern California, not far from where I grew up. The resort is right on the beach, a very inspirational setting.

On a Friday a couple of weeks later, Steve rode with me to Pajaro in my Porsche (a car I've loved for its great design since I was 13). During the drive, he told me, "The team is enthusiastic about what they're doing, but that's not enough." He wanted to get them so fired up that they would work beyond what they even thought they were capable of.

I offered some thoughts that didn't get much response, and then I said, "Here's an idea you might want think about. *Vision* is motivational. When you talk about going someplace and you're looking way ahead to the future, that's what people get excited about. When John Kennedy said we were going to put a man on the moon, that was motivational." I told him that what would really get the team fired up was a vision that extended way into the future.

At the off-site, when he got up to make his opening remarks, we all saw a Steve none of us had seen before. He was so inspirational, so moving.

He said the Macintosh would be the beginning of an incredible journey, growing out of the technology the team was developing. They weren't just building a groundbreaking computer; they were creating a cornerstone for the world of tomorrow. Some people sit in church and feel that God is talking to them. I had something of that same feeling: Steve was like a god standing on a mountaintop. A glance around the room showed me that the others were as caught up in the moment as I was.

He had taken the kernel of the idea I suggested and, in that distinctive, almost eerily insightful way of his, made it his own.

It was the first time I saw him pulling the team together and building enthusiasm. He felt it so passionately that he almost had tears in his eyes. I could feel a wave of emotion soaking the room. I had never seen more than one or two people in my life who had that kind of impact on others.

During the two days of the off-site, team members talked about the details of what they were doing, how it was going, and what the challenges were. But Steve had shaped the mood and gotten everyone fired up with his opening remarks, not talking about the short-term goals, but about the long-term *vision*. People left there *so* excited.

That's how you get people excited: offer a long-term vision. But it needs to come from true passion. Faking it, just mouthing the words, doesn't fool anyone. It's building an environment that makes everyone feel they are surrounded by equally talented people and that their work collectively is bigger than the contribution of any individual team member.

Vision and Passion Are More Important than Credentials

About five months after joining Apple, I pressed Steve for a conversation about his views on the principles of leadership. He asked me to his house one evening. Throughout his early adult life, Steve lived in homes almost bare of furniture, a result, I believe, of his embracing Buddhism after a trip to India in his early 20s. In one bare room of his house in Los Gatos, near Cupertino, Steve discussed how industry needed to recognize that innovation could come from any place, and how managers, leaders, and entrepreneurs had to change the ways innovation is encouraged and practiced. This kind of thinking is widely accepted now (even if not widely practiced), but at the time it was exciting and radical.

Steve also offered some reflections that were the opposite of the prevailing management wisdom I had learned. "It's not my job to pull things together from different parts of the company and clear the ways to get resources for the key projects," he said. "It's my job to push the team and make them even better, coming up with more aggressive visions of how it could be."

We also talked about something he was holding me accountable for: how to communicate to the Macintosh team the way that Steve intended to practice innovation. My suggestion was that his ideas would stick better if he communicated them with powerful metaphors and storytelling.

I left there that night and was struck by a thought: *I've been studying leadership for years at college, for 10 years at IBM, and then at Intel, but I'm hearing brilliant concepts I've never heard before. How did this 27-year-old come to these insights?* Even more, I thought, *Wow, this guy is a visionary. But even better, he's a captivating storyteller. How great is that?!*

What further struck me afterward was how the conversation changed my views of my own leadership capabilities. In my previous positions with IBM, I had always been on the fast track—pegged as someone who might have the potential to become a vice president of the company. But I never really believed that could ever happen. I was a farm boy from California; most of the other fast-trackers were Eastern born and educated at one or another of America's great universities like Harvard, Yale, Cornell, or MIT. Thinking back later about that evening with Steve, I came for the first time to believe that leadership isn't about your pedigree but rather about you, the individual. It's about your beliefs and your personal commitment to your own vision. I took away with me from that conversation something I have believed ever since: that leadership is not something intuitive, not something you're born with. Rather, if you're open to it, it's something you learn from life.

When I was 14 years old, I built a sailboat called a pram from a kit. On the water, I learned to tie knots, to read the wind, and became a very good sailor. Later in life, I sailed in a race to Hawaii with some very seasoned and well-trained sailors, and by the end of the race I had become the second mate, with no formal training. I had become an intuitive sailor. Steve-style leadership is the same way. The most important ingredient is not an MBA but passion and a vision.

Vision Must Be Based on Your Customers

Looking back, it's amazing to me that Steve Jobs, even in the earliest days, understood that every powerful business vision has to focus on the customer experience, not just lowest cost or most impressive technology or other isolated competitive advantages.

The prime example: When Steve first saw the computer mouse, he immediately got it. He immediately understood that all of the computer experience could be controlled by the user by means of the mouse, and that the user interface would provide the most important leverage for giving customers quick and easy access for learning and using the computer.

Another example: The Apple II was completely loved by a passionate group of teachers at every level, but especially through grade 12. It was the first computer they could bring into their classrooms for their students to use. The early Apple product shows, for some reason called Harvest Feasts, were heavily attended by teachers. Steve never forgot the teachers' enthusiasm, and it showed in Apple's later success in the education market.

Vision and Your Vendors

A compelling vision isn't just motivating to employees: It should move your vendors and other partners as well. In some cases, if it doesn't, you're better off without them.

One of my favorite experiences on this topic involved a disk-drive company that wanted to become an Apple vendor. They were invited to come in to demo their drives, and the visitors set up their demo using IBM MS-DOS computers. When Steve arrived, he took two steps in the room, saw the competitor's machines, turned, and walked out without saying a word. His silence was deafening. No more needed to be said.

After I had been at Apple for some time, I was asked to take over the IT organization, in addition to my other functions. On my first tour, I was shocked to see that all the work involving Apple's finances and sales was being done on IBM computers. IBM—Apple's biggest competitor and enemy. I ordered that the IBM machines be replaced with DEC computers. If that vice president didn't have enough loyalty to use Apple's own products, he failed the vision challenge. He had demonstrated that he hadn't understood the Apple values.

Acquiring a Company Can Water Down Your Vision and Culture

One trap that a great many companies fall into lies in acquiring a new company without first making sure that the culture of the company being acquired is a good match for the culture of your own firm. This was another strength of Steve Jobs: He always showed very good judgment about whether to hire people who had the particular technological expertise he was looking for or, instead, to license the technology or acquire the entire company.

He had been on the other end of that equation when he left Apple and was running NeXT. Apple was in need of a new operating system, and the NeXTStep operating system that Steve's software engineers had developed was one of the leading candidates. Apple could have just licensed NeXTStep or purchased the technology outright. But the Apple CEO at the time, Gil Amelio, saw that by buying not just the software but the entire company, Apple would acquire the services of many talented software engineers— people who had created the NeXT operating system and would be the best qualified to rewrite the software to run on the Mac. So that's what Gil did: he offered Steve a deal to buy not just the software but the entire company—acquiring the technology, the entire staff that had been so carefully assembled, and Steve himself.

It was a well-reasoned decision. Steve and Gil both understood that the culture of NeXT was identical to the original culture of Apple—because Steve had created them both. It turned out to be a brilliant decision for Steve, who was soon back in the driver's seat, this time running all of Apple Computer, instead of just one product group. But it was also a brilliant decision for Apple: the company would not have achieved greatness without the guidance and culture of cofounder Steve.

To me, it's a mystery how smart people at the head of major companies, in making an acquisition, so often undervalue the importance of cultural fit.

Communicating the Vision

As Steve put it after his return to Apple, following the dark years when the company seemed to have lost its way, "This is not a one-man show. What's reinvigorating this company is two things: One, there's a lot of really talented people [here] who listened to the world tell them they were losers for a couple of years, and some of them were on the verge of starting to believe it themselves. But they're not losers. What they didn't have was a good set of coaches, a good plan. But they have that now."[1]

That was Steve, in the process of putting a strong vision in place and making sure that every Apple employee understood it.

Of course people need frequent reminders and inspiration to live by the team vision. A daily e-mail to the team? Quarterly off-sites?

What other ways can you think of to keep the vision in front of your people?

The Way It's Made Can Be a Part of the Vision

One of Steve's heroes, American car pioneer Henry Ford, not only changed society by making automobiles inexpensive enough for the masses but along the way demonstrated that large-scale mass manufacturing was possible. Ford didn't invent the assembly line (it's said that he picked up the idea from a visit to a slaughterhouse!) but he was the first to use the technique in large factories, where workers were able to turn out a car at the astounding pace of better than one an hour. (A comparison isn't entirely fair since today's cars are vastly more complex but, a century later, the production rate is only twice as fast.)

So, when Steve began dreaming of creating a new, automated factory to build the Macintosh, there was a lot of Henry Ford embedded in the dream. Steve was driven in part by a concern about the ability of the existing Apple manufacturing system to be competitive in building Macs. But beyond that, it was a cultural issue, a matter of national pride: He was very concerned about the fact that the Japanese were becoming the manufacturing kings of the world. In fact, when the Mac factory became a topic of buzz in 1982, even Apple Computer was having over 60 percent of its products manufactured outside the United States. Besides Steve's drive to be personally in charge of every aspect of bringing the Macintosh to life that he could, his dream of having a *Made in the USA* label on the Macs was a powerful part of his vision for the Macintosh. (In fact, the claim was a stretch: The components would actually be manufactured in a number of different countries and shipped to the Apple factory. *Assembled in the USA* would have been a more valid claim.)

Steve knew that based on labor costs, the only way to compete with Japan for manufacturing was through an automated system. And he intended for the factory to be run by Macintoshes, as well—an idea that hardly anyone who understood automated factories thought would be possible. So the Mac factory faced a lot of challenges. But Steve never hid from challenges.

The design called for a fully automated factory, from the receiving dock to the shipping dock, and for having a staff of no more than 100 people. When the first Macs began rolling off the assembly line every 24 seconds, with the entire process controlled by Macs, I was very happy and proud for Steve.

Giving Your Team a Special Identity

Some months after I had joined Apple, Steve and I were discussing the final steps in readying a building for the Mac team to move into—a building of their own. (Among my other duties, I was also responsible for the facilities group at Apple—convenient for Steve so he could readily give me his architectural inputs; yes, of course, he held strong opinions and had well-developed taste about architecture, as well.) He told me about his recent dinner with the incredibly talented advertising man who had become Steve's esteemed friend, Jay Chiat of Chiat/Day Advertising. He and Chiat, Steve said, had come up with the answer regarding how to re-energize the culture of the Macintosh development team. He gave me the concept in a single word: Pirates.

And then he gave me the rest of it: "Pirates! Not The Navy."

He wasn't looking for my approval on this one, but I chimed in anyway: "Wow—brilliant!" It reflected all the attributes we wanted to convey. This turned out to be a remarkably suitable time for announcing a shift in culture. The early Mac team members had begun to complain that the organization was getting too big and that it was starting to feel bureaucratic. The Mac team had begun as rebellious, and now we were seeing it grow more like The Navy every day.

Steve didn't mention the Pirates idea to anyone else, holding onto it until another off-site, this one at the La Playa Hotel in Carmel—once again near a sandy beach on the Pacific Ocean.

At the first meeting, each team member entering the room was greeted by a staffer handing out a sweatshirt emblazoned with the logo

PIRATES! NOT THE NAVY

For Steve, this meeting came at a time of special urgency. Apple had just introduced the Lisa personal computer, positioned as the company's first breakaway product, the first one that was totally different from the company's breadwinner, the Apple II. Steve wanted to save the Macintosh from what he perceived as the Lisa's mistakes. In his view, the Lisa group had become very political and very bureaucratic, and had lost the ability to create a paradigm-changing product. They had become The Navy.

Worse, he was convinced that the whole company was going in the same direction. Apple had started to slip into a standard corporate structure. The start-up mentality that had made Apple so successful seemed to be fading. The only path to save the company was developing a truly innovative product. And the only way to create a truly innovative product was by turning the Macintosh team into a true Pirate organization.

On the first day of the Carmel session, Steve explained that Mac was now a Pirate organization and what that meant. The tone and direction of the Mac group was set.

The Mac group had grown to more than 40 people by this time and solidifying the team was critical. Particularly since at the meeting we established the first ship date for the Mac: May 1983, only slightly more than a year away. This was the first meeting of the whole team where the complete product was discussed—from prototypes, to software, to marketing, to sales. The goal had been set, so making sure we were all onboard was critical.

When the crew left Carmel at the end of the meeting to return to Cupertino, no one had any doubt that we were Pirates, and Steve Jobs was the Pirate captain.

The Magical World of the Pirate Life

The Pirates of the Macintosh team lived with a similar range of emotions. The day-to-day work was grueling because of the unbelievably tight deadlines and because Steve, the Pirate captain, was often not satisfied, demanding the work just accomplished be done over and done better or even differently because he had come up with a new idea he liked even more. As the launch date neared, some of the software engineers took to grabbing a bit of sleep under their desks, then rousing themselves and getting back to work—never going home for a full night's sleep.

And yet, despite the pressures and demands, there was a feeling of being privileged to be part of the team, a joyous sense that you were doing something you would always look back on as an experience never to be duplicated. People couldn't wait to get to work. There was a unique, nearly magical sense of exhilaration.

That's the kind of Pirate work environment that good managers try to create—the kind where people do the best work they have ever done.

Flying a Flag

When you give a team a distinctive identity, magic can happen. Steve had created a special aura that made every individual on the Macintosh team feel they were contributing to something unique.

One aspect of what the Mac team was achieving that we didn't recognize at the time had to do with the term *heroes*. Probably coined by some long-forgotten journalist, the most brilliant innovators of Silicon Valley had come to be crowned by having this word attached to them. But the term had been applied almost exclusively to innovators on the hardware side. One of the most overlooked aspects about what made the Macintosh so unique was its many *software* innovations. Over time, several of the team's greatest contributors on the software side would start being referred to as software heroes.

One day, one of those future software heroes, Steve Capps, had a flash of inspiration: If the Mac team was a band of Pirates, their building should fly a Pirate flag. He bought some black cloth, sewed it into a flag, and asked Mac graphics designer Susan Kare to paint a big skull and crossbones in white at the center.

The timing was perfect. That decision by Steve several months earlier that the Mac team should have their own building, to make them even more clearly separated from The Navy bureaucracy of the rest of Apple, had just come to fruition: The building conversion had just been completed and everything was ready for the troops to arrive. (Though Steve Jobs' day-to-day work involved running one small development team within a $150 million company, by this time he also wore a second hat as Apple's board chairman, and so had the clout to decide what building the Macintosh team would occupy.)

Steve Capps had his flag ready the weekend before the team was to take possession of their new quarters. On Sunday night, while a few supporters watched from the street, Capps climbed onto the roof with the flag. He found a few long rusty nails, which he used to secure a makeshift rod as a flagpole with the Pirate flag at the top, ready to greet the Mac team members as they arrived for work the next morning.

The flag caused a sensation. The Mac team took it as a symbol and an inspiration (although many in The Navy parts of Apple took it as something of an insult).

For me personally, the flag was both an inspiration and a challenge. Most weekday mornings as I drove down Bandley Drive toward my office, the sight of that flag waving in the morning breeze would bring a proud little smile. Yet at the same time, as VP of human resources, I kept asking myself, *How do I get the rest of Apple into the Pirate mentality?*

It wasn't to happen until Steve left the company and then returned.

Vision for Innovation

From the early Macintosh days, one of Steve's favorite lines about innovation was, "The system is that there is no system." We had processes, of course, but he was fierce about not permitting processes that got in the way of innovation.

Steve expanded on this in a brilliant 2004 conversation with *BusinessWeek* computer editor Peter Burrows. He told Burrows, "[I]nnovation comes from people meeting up in the hallways or calling each other at 10:30 at night with a new idea, or because they realized something that shoots holes in how we've been thinking about a problem. It's ad hoc meetings of six people called by someone who thinks he has figured out the coolest new thing ever and who wants to know what other people think of his idea."[2]

Over the years, many journalists and writers have emphasized the negatives of Steve Jobs' management style, strong personality, and ways of handling people. Despite his many successes, or perhaps because of them, Steve was widely seen as a controversial leader. One blogger on the Harvard

Business School website, Bill Taylor, captured the sentiment: "In terms of his approach to leadership, Jobs represents . . . well, if not the worst, then certainly not something worth emulating."[3]

My perspective, having worked with him on a daily basis, is different. Yes, he was often difficult, certainly controversial, but when you have the privilege of working for a visionary genius, you don't let hurt feelings get in the way.

Besides, this was the man who was honored as the "CEO of the Decade" by America's leading business magazine, *Fortune*. And obviously the performance of Apple reflects his amazing leadership.

I would have worked for Steve Jobs any time, any place, and I believe that's true for most of the people who have worked closely with him.

2

Steve's Business Philosophy and Values

Being the richest man in the cemetery doesn't matter to me. Going to bed at night saying we've done something wonderful, that's what matters to me.

—Steve Jobs

Steve and I spent a lot of time discussing the core of the company's values. He kept emphasizing that they had to reflect the nature of a *start-up* company and of a company driven by innovation, entrepreneurship, and products that truly satisfied the user. He wanted the company to be based on values, and he wanted values that would remind everyone not to compromise the integrity of the product in the name of profit. He wanted the company to be an innovator and a premier manufacturer of personal computers—but as the *value* leader, not the price leader.

He also wanted the statement to be based on two further premises:

Achieving our goals is important to us.
We are equally concerned with the way we reach those goals.

We had long discussions about what should be included in a values statement for Apple. What I came up with, following his guidance, was a document that began by stating the business principles and then presented a set of values.

The *business principles* included these items:

- To follow the principles of human engineering to build "friendly" products whose simplicity and ease of use make them natural extensions of their owners.
- To create a worldwide customer service organization to service retailers, distributors, and technical support centers, unmatched in the industry.

When we had finished our work, the set of *values* included these:

- Value 1—Empathy for the users

  Offer superior products that fill real needs and provide lasting value. We are interested in solving customer problems, while not compromising ethics or integrity in the name of profit.

- Value 2—Aggressiveness

  Set aggressive goals and drive ourselves hard to achieve them. Recognize this is a unique time when our products will change the way people work and live.

- Value 3—Positive social contribution

  Make a positive social contribution. As a corporate citizen, we should be an economic, intellectual, and social asset in communities where we operate. But beyond that we expect to make this world a better place to live. We build products that extend human capability.

- Value 4—Innovation and Vision

  Innovation and Vision to build our company by providing products that are new and needed. We accept the risk inherent in following our vision and work to develop leadership products.

- Value 5—Individual performance

  We expect individual commitment and performance above the standard for industry. Only then can we make profits that permit the investment in other corporate objectives.

- Value 6—Team spirit

  Teamwork is essential to the success of Apple, for each job is too big to be done by only one person. Individuals are encouraged to interact with all levels of management, sharing ideas and suggestions to improve Apple's effectiveness and our contribution to quality of life.

- Value 7—Quality

  We care about what we do. We build into Apple products a level of quality, performance, and value to earn the respect and loyalty of our customers.

- Value 8—Individual reward

  We recognize each person's contribution to Apple's success and we share the financial rewards that flow from high performance. We recognize that rewards must be psychological as well as financial and strive for an atmosphere where each individual can share the adventure and excitement of working at Apple.

- Value 9—Great management

  The attitudes of a manager toward people are of primary importance. Employees should be able to trust the motives and integrity of their supervisors. It is the responsibility of management to create a productive environment where Apple values flourish.

These values became part of everyday communication and a standard by which employees could measure how they themselves and their management were performing.

Recognizing the Need for a Values Statement

How did Apple, still a young company, come to recognize the need for a values statement? Most young companies don't have a written set of corporate values that lay the groundwork for the culture of the company. There are so many key things that need to get done all at the same time, just for the company to survive, that writing down a set of values seems like a back-burner item.

At Apple, the motivation for creating values guidelines arose out of a negative incident. On February 25, 1981, when the company had been in business for only five years, then-CEO Mike "Scotty" Scott looked out the window of his office early one afternoon and saw about 30 Apple people outside, hanging around, chatting. Nothing unusual about that—when they were struggling over some thorny problem, pairs or whole teams of engineers, in particular, often hung around in the fresh air while they batted ideas back and forth. I have no doubts that many technical problems were probably solved in just that way. On that particular day, Scotty for some reason didn't read that scene as *Engineers at work* but, I guess, as something like *People standing around wasting the company's money*. He had been frustrated with the failure of the Apple III, blamed mismanagement for this failure, and wanted to make a point. He decided to do that by firing some people.

There was no economic reason for this. Apple was growing at a frenzied pace, with sales booming and plenty of cash in the bank.

Scotty advised board chairman Mike Markkula and the other board members what he wanted to do but didn't wait for their response. In what would become known in the corridors of Apple and in the Apple histories as Black Wednesday, he started calling people into his office and telling them, one by one, that they were being let go—about 30 people in all, among them some very talented engineers.

It was a bad decision and had quick consequences. As a result of this bizarre action, the top jobs of the company were reshuffled. Mike Markkula took over as president, Steve Jobs as chairman (his title had been VP of technology), and Mike Scott left the company soon after.

In the aftermath, a task force was formed to put together and set down on paper a statement of Apple's values.

The Worldwide Culture

It was critical that this culture of Apple values become a worldwide system—so every Apple employee, in every office, in every country would be in tune with the values that had been set at Apple headquarters in Cupertino. This was accomplished by making values indoctrination a part of the process for new hires in all countries and a refresher in leadership training seminars for new Apple managers. The values document became part of the fabric of the company.

In human resources, I made it one of the key responsibilities of the HR people to make sure the values were being adhered to on a daily basis, and I was to be advised of any deviations. I had listening posts all over the world, and the information I received was key to making this an accountable value system.

When executives from Cupertino would travel, we made it a key part of their job to discuss and monitor how values were being implemented in all parts of the world. Since in the early days I spent a lot of my time in Europe and Asia, I was able to make sure that the value system was being adhered to in Paris and Tokyo as it was in New York and Cleveland. At any Apple facility Steve and I visited, we would go on walk-throughs and in casual discussions with employees bring up the question, "How are the values doing here?"

I also created Apple Corporate TV. All employee meetings we would have in Cupertino would be available via satellite in Apple offices around the world.

Believing in the power of the pen, I also established an official Apple newspaper for all employees. Adapting the name of the street in Cupertino that the Apple buildings were located on, Bandley Drive, we called the new publication the *Bandley Shuffle*, or the BS for short. (That abbreviation was typical Apple irreverence and brought smiles.)

The unique thing about the *Bandley Shuffle* was that the editor I hired from a newspaper was given the authority to run any article without getting management approval for content, as required in almost every other company I know about. Of course, the editor understood that the contents had to be in line with Apple values, but beyond that, he had a free hand.

The Lack of Secrecy in the Early Apple

All companies have secrets, of course. The origin of Apple's culture of secrecy isn't hard to understand. When the first Macintosh was in the late stages of development, some reporters knew many of the details. Writers such as the prominent technology journalist John Dvorak published inside knowledge of the Mac configuration, as well as business decisions and even conversations from Mac team meetings, before many Apple employees heard these details. Even Apple people in the know would grab up Dvorak's latest column to see if he had any tidbits they hadn't heard yet. So it didn't surprise anyone that Microsoft and Sony had extensive knowledge about the Mac before it was unveiled.

Steve became so frustrated by the leaks that he had our main conference room swept for hidden microphones. He and I came up with a plan to expose one Mac team member we thought might be slipping stories to Dvorak. We concocted some bits of misinformation, which I casually mentioned to the suspect. Dvorak never published those details, so our man wasn't the snitch, after all. (If he ever found out we had suspected him, I hereby apologize for our mistrust.)

I ran into Dvorak some 10 years later and said, "Okay, who was it?"

He didn't have to ask what I was talking about. His response was, "It wasn't one person. There were many." So Apple had been like a sieve, leaking from many places.

The truth is that even Steve himself would sometimes curry favor with a particular reporter by whispering some supposedly secret tidbit to him. He gave rise to a saying that began to be heard around the corridors of the company: "Apple is the only ship that leaks from the top."

All that would change quite drastically—a subject we'll come back to later.

A Background in Business Values

I had come to Apple already well aware of the power of values. At IBM I had seen a value system that was amazingly powerful and was a guiding light for the operation of the company. It was the underpinning of a very strong culture and, I was convinced, had helped the company become so successful: in terms of market capitalization, IBM was ranked number 6 in the world and was the only nonunion company among the top 135 companies globally.

I have always felt the IBM success was, in particular, largely the result of several key aspects of the culture. Among them *respect for the individual* and the *open-door policy* have always seemed especially key. (The open-door policy referred to the practice of being able to approach any executive in the company with a problem or suggestion, including going to the chairman of the board with an issue.) I used to marvel that every man in the 300,000-person IBM workforce would put on a white shirt and a tie every morning—that one simple fact showing the dedication that can come from adhering to shared values.

But I was aware of one big problem with IBM's values: most of them were not written down. It was like England, where the people speak proudly of their constitution, though there is no such written document.

Companies with Values that Steve Admired

Though I came to Apple already admiring IBM's values, I learned to admire one other company as well. Steve was always very impressed with Sony. In our visits to Japan and meetings with the company's CEO and cofounder, Akio Morita, we were always struck by the remarkable attitude of all of Sony's employees. We talked a lot about how Sony kept its entrepreneurial and product-orientation spirit alive. How did they communicate their values?

It was interesting to Steve and me that they did not have a values statement. Rather, it was part of the Japanese culture to be completely committed to one's company and job. It was not specified in a document; they just lived it. But Sony did underpin the culture by providing its employees with certain perks that supported who they were.

Samsung on the other hand did have a written values statement. A few of the items were these:

People—A company is its people. At Samsung, we're dedicated to giving our people a wealth of opportunities to reach their full potential.

Excellence—Everything we do at Samsung is driven by an unyielding passion for excellence.

Change—Change is constant and innovation is critical to a company's survival.

Integrity—Operating in an ethical way is the foundation of Samsung.

Co-prosperity—A business cannot be successful unless it creates prosperity and opportunity for others.

Losing Ground

Culture informs success, not the other way around. And leadership drives culture. After Steve left Apple, CEO John Sculley realized it was critically important to make sure the employees of Apple felt that the management change would not affect the future of the company. At the grass roots of Apple, the culture that had been established in 1981 was alive and very strong. Still, it needed to be reinforced.

As vice president of human resources, I had the challenge of figuring out how to refresh the Apple culture. For all his drawbacks, Steve had nonetheless established a culture that made Apple a place where you felt appreciated and rewarded even though it was a demanding place to work.

Shortly after Steve's departure, I met with John, the other executives, and the board of directors and made a presentation that became known as Apple's "Stakeholders' Report." This outlined a plan to create stronger communication about the Apple values and to make sure the values were reinforced and adhered to. This was critical to the company's future.

It was also at this meeting that I suggested, "One Apple messiah is gone. We need to bring the other one back." It was a plea to get Steve Wozniak involved again. John Sculley immediately left the room and called Woz, who agreed to accept a role with the company.

I put into place a daily "Breakfast Club" meeting that became famous—getting all the key executives together at 7 AM every morning to keep everyone completely updated. To deal with gossip and any troubling rumors and to answer questions, I also launched the Hearsay Café—making an Apple executive available in the cafeteria at certain announced times, so any employee, without feeling pressure, could get questions answered.

John Sculley understood the power of the Apple culture and knew that one of the secrets to his success in managing Apple was going to be to fully support and adhere to the culture. He knew that the Apple culture was one of the key drivers of results and that its importance should not be underestimated.

In 1985, sales and profits declined and Apple experienced the first losing quarter in its history. In a massive layoff, John ordered that 1,200 people from around the world be let go. As I prepared the 1985 Annual Report, John gave me a statement to be included, saying in part, "It's remarkable that we accomplished a reorganization and managed to respect the human dignity of those who left and at same time cultivating the spirit of those who remained. Jay really cares about people, the environment in which they work, the integrity of the values they share, and the importance of giving Apple people the opportunity for personal growth. Apple could not have grown up so fast without this."

I appreciated the praise, but it did not forestall a future locking of horns between John and me.

The Head Pirate Returns

While Steve was running NeXT, he and I had a conversation that I thought odd at the time. Now, though, I understand.

His conversation was all about Apple. It was clear he was keeping very closely in touch with what was going on, showing a lot more knowledge about the internal workings than he could have learned from reading newspaper and magazine articles. Talking as if he was still at Apple, he complained that the products were bad, and buyers didn't have the old passion for the company and its products. He complained there were too many products and that it was a mistake to try to turn out products for every market group—personal, education, business, and so on. And he complained that the computer stores still stocked Apple products in the corner, practically out of sight, because dealers could make more money selling Windows machines.

Later, when Steve returned to Apple and was named the interim CEO, nobody had any doubt the culture was going to be changing. He had several key priorities. Foremost, get the organization back to being focused on *product*. Then find the right talent, organize those people in small teams, and restructure the product lines. In a very short period of time, Steve was able to reorganize the company in his flat, small-team, direct-communication Pirate style—all with a focus on the product.

Meanwhile, a Jobsian e-mail went out banning all smoking anywhere on the Apple campus. One employee ran into Steve, introduced himself, and introduced his dog; five minutes later, another e-mail: dogs no longer allowed. Nobody wanted to step onto an elevator and encounter Steve, who was asking people, "What have you done today to earn what I'm paying you?" A rumor circulated that someone had been fired for not presenting an acceptable answer during one of those elevator rides—though nobody could ever put a name to such a person. Still, people who never exercised began using the stairs.

In March 1998, to concentrate on a simple product plan that is the essence of a creative, innovative operation, Steve cancelled a number of products, including the Newton, a ground-breaking early PDA that even including handwriting recognition. Newton sales had just turned the corner; the product was beginning to make money for the company. Some thought Steve was crazy for cancelling what promised to turn into a highly profitable item. He didn't care: Apple's core product was computers, and he knew that's what he needed to get the company focused on. Computers and nothing else. That would change later, of course, but not until he had returned the company to good health.

With the help of Apple's chief designer, Jony (pronounced *Johnny*) Ive, Steve shook his innovation wand to usher in a new look for personal computers, making the new Macs in their own way as distinctive as the very first one had been. While work was progressing on major software and hardware innovations, Steve had his troops gin up some signs that the company was turning a corner. Some of the new Macs came in candy colors, others in gleaming metals with rounded edges. He wanted to show proof of innovation, and it was happening.

I've lost track of who originally described Steve as living by the adage that "cool products demand cool pitches." When he rejoined Apple, the company had more than a dozen ad agencies. He fired them all except for the team at Chiat/Day, the company that had created the "1984" commercial.

The agency came through again with another campaign that made advertising history: "Think Different." (Grammatical English would have been "Think Differently," but it didn't have the same punch; the intentional error didn't interfere with the campaign winning many major advertising awards.) The ads were built around large pictures of famous people who had achieved great things because they were able to "think different." The hope was that these people were so famous that the giant posters and the magazine ads did not need to bear their names: you were expected to recognize their faces. Many of the people were chosen by Steve himself. The selection included scientist Albert Einstein, Martin Luther King Jr., architect Frank Lloyd Wright, and John Lennon of the Beatles, as well as Steve's personal music hero, Bob Dylan.

Building on the Values

One of the big advantages for Steve after his return was the power of the Apple values. At the grass roots, the culture that had been established in 1981 was still alive and strong, despite all the changes in top management. Steve took advantage of the Apple workers who had been longing for his return to lead them out of troubled waters.

The standard version of the company's financial condition at the time, according to Walter Isaacson and just about everyone else, is that the company was on the verge of bankruptcy. It's the version that Steve preferred everyone to believe. Yet the truth is that Apple had some $1.5 billion in the bank—vastly more than enough to purchase NeXT while at the same time enriching Steve to the tune of 1.5 million Apple shares.

True, the products weren't selling well and the company was bleeding cash, but there was more than enough cash on hand to give Steve time to get the company back on track. If Apple really had been weeks from filing bankruptcy, he never would have agreed to take control. Being in command of Apple when the company had to go out of business was the last thing he would ever have chosen to do.

As his early plan of action, Steve could have focused on touting all the products that were then in the Apple lineup. Instead he focused on renewing Apple's original start-up culture. He did this by focusing on three basic things.

First, rethink the product strategy: instead of marketing a multitude of products, he wanted to decide which ones were really true to Apple's core business and would be shutting down some product lines, even though they were generating revenue.

Second, put in place a cohesive strategy to end executive and manager infighting. When new ideas are forming and exceptionally bright people wrestle with difficult problems together, there are going to be disagreements. Out of this tension, complicated ideas get born and take shape. Steve wanted to make sure that any conflict would be dealt with up front and in positive ways, rather than allowing conflicts to fester, which too often leads to destructive behaviors.

And third, achieve a cross-disciplinary view of how the company should operate. He was looking for a positive atmosphere of teamwork across the company at every level, from product concept to sales.

Steve's Most Important Value: Attention to Details

Each of us has our own set of values, our own sense of what is important. If you have read other articles or books about Steve Jobs, you already know that at the top of his list of priorities was a compelling sense that attention to even the smallest details is crucial. Anyone involved in product development could hardly pick a more important value to have at the top of his or her own list.

On our walks together, one frequent subject was design, which, he complained, most people understood as how something *looks* but really should be understood as referring to the product as a whole. This was the first time I heard him express the concept that design means how it looks, but more important, it also means how it *works*.

Once, music-industry CEO Hilary Rosen was allowed to sit in on a session when two Apple team members were showing Steve their new version of a screen display that Steve had rejected on the previous go-around. "Steve spent about twenty minutes back and forth with the engineers about the best place within a three square inch section to put three words," the CEO reported later in a private conversation. "He was *that* focused on the details of the design."[1]

Journalist Tim Scannell once sat down with Steve to do an interview. Halfway through his first question, Steve put up his hand and interrupted to ask what he knew about—of all things—washing machines. Like most of us, the journalist didn't know much more than how to load them and turn them on. He later wrote that over the next 10 to 15 minutes, Steve talked washing machines, "and I learned more about the man and his intense curiosity and zest for knowledge than I did about any washday miracles."[2]

That must have been about the same time that Steve also did an interview with Gary Wolf of *Wired* magazine, because he still had washing machines on his mind. Steve regaled the writer with a story about how his whole family had been involved in the selection of a new washing machine and dryer. "We spent some time in our family talking about what's the trade-off we want to make. We spent about two weeks talking about this. Every night at the dinner table we'd get around to that old washer-dryer discussion." In the end, the decision came down to a choice between Miele machines (pronounced *Mee-luh*), made in Germany, or an American brand. Steve told the journalist that the American machines took about half as long to wash the clothes but that, in his view, the machines made by Miele "did a much better job, used about one-quarter as much water, and treated the clothes more gently so they would last longer." (Of course, Steve, for his part, dressed the same way almost every day and owned probably a hundred of his favorite black turtleneck shirts and ditto for his favorite brand of jeans. So how long it took for the laundry to be finished was never going to be one of his challenges.)

In the end, they chose the Miele. At today's prices, Miele washers sell in the neighborhood of $3,000, compared to machines from American companies that are available in the $300 to $600 price range. Steve explained to the journalist that the Mieles were "too expensive, but that's just because nobody buys them in this country."

Of course, the conversation around the Jobs' dinner table wasn't really about washing machines; it was about passing along his sense of the importance of design to his children. And he obviously thought the message had gotten through. He told the journalist that the new machines were "one of the few products we've bought over the last few years that we're all really happy about." And perhaps it's not surprising for a man so focused on design that he finished the story by saying, "I got more thrill out of them than I have out of any piece of high tech in years."[3]

So there's a challenge for each of us: be able to relate a story that so vividly captures one of the values we prize.

Power of the User Culture

It's not enough that the values and culture of a company are embraced by the employees; they also need to be a reflection of the company's customers. Walk into any Apple store and you can see and feel the Apple culture at work.

The same is true of some other values-oriented companies. Consider Starbucks: They have a published set of values that every employee is expected to know, understand, and follow—and their values statement is very customer oriented. I especially admire the way that the wording goes beyond pedestrian, everyday language, as shown by these excerpts:

> Our mission is to inspire and nurture the human spirit—one person, one cup and one neighborhood at a time.

> We're passionate about ethically sourcing the finest coffee beans, roasting them with great care, and improving the lives of people who grow them. We care deeply about all of this; our work is never done.

And about the customers:

> When we are fully engaged, we connect with, laugh with, and uplift the lives of our customers—even if just for a few moments. Sure, it starts with the promise of a perfectly made beverage, but our work goes far beyond that. It's really about human connection.

If you were to visit the Apple campus, one of the things you would likely find striking is the evidence of how committed the employees are to the Apple products. You would see that every Apple staffer carries an iPhone, has a MacBook or MacBook Pro, and has an iPad. If you are an observant person, you would likely conclude from the intensity on their faces and the bounce in their steps that they are extraordinarily committed and extraordinarily enthusiastic about their work.

That cannot be said about the workers in most companies, although I have observed similar attitudes in the employees of companies like Google, Oracle, and, yes, even Microsoft. Bravo for them—companies with a strong and well-defined values system are the kinds of places we all want to work.

3

People Who Know More than You

Choosing and Leading Your Lieutenants

A lot of people in our industry haven't had very diverse experiences. So they don't have enough dots to connect, and they end up with very linear solutions without a broad perspective on the problem. The broader one's understanding of the human experience, the better design we will have.

—Steve Jobs

I mentioned earlier how I met Steve Jobs for the first time when he started a conversation with me in a restaurant, and after a few minutes of chat told me I should come to work for him. What I didn't understand at the time was that the whole conversation, from the moment he learned I had been in management at IBM and Intel, was really a job interview—an unusual one.

Any other interviewer would have asked me, "Why did you leave IBM?" Steve instead asked, "What did you think about IBM?" I answered that IBM was set on a plan to control all the computer rooms in the world, and they did not see the value of personal computing. "In my first meeting with Mr. Watson," I told Steve, "I tried to make the case that personal computing had a great future and IBM ought to be pursuing it. He said he agreed that was true. He didn't actually say the company wasn't going to adopt the idea, but told me I needed to be patient."

But I also told Steve that I thought IBM was a great company, a very solid business, from development to sales, and that "I learned a lot about global business planning and operations."

I mentioned that I had been fortunate enough to meet company CEO Tom Watson Jr. through a letter I sent him, and found him to be a great business leader and an open thinker. Months later I found out that Steve silently regarded Mr. Watson as one of his heroes. So it turned out to be a happy remark: it suggested to Steve that he and I might hold similar views in some areas that mattered a great deal to him.

He brought up the topic of moving computing out of the computer room and into the hands of the user. Steve wasn't just making conversation, of course. Again he was casually testing me—throwing out an idea to see how I would respond. He asked, "Why do you think IBM hasn't seen the power of this?"

The toughest question he asked was, "Why weren't you successful in making IBM see this vision? Didn't they have confidence in your ideas?"

Steve also asked me about Intel and my opinion of Intel cofounder Andy Grove. "I went to Intel thinking it was still a start-up operation," I answered. "But it wasn't."

I immediately realized that it must have sounded like I hadn't done very good research on Intel before accepting a job there. Steve, though, didn't seem at all put off by my response. I went on to say that I had admired Andy as a great leader but didn't like his dictatorial style. And that I had wanted to work for a company that was interested in tapping the consumer market, but Andy's focus was limited to running a hardware-producing technology company. Again my answer must have resonated: Apple was involved in a running feud with Intel.

Steve was looking for someone who fit his criterion for business wisdom. I would realize only much later what a compliment it was to be offered a job by Steve: it meant that I had met his very demanding standards.

The lesson is that the best hiring results come when you're picky, almost as if choosing a girlfriend or boyfriend, a husband or wife. You need to light each other's fires. The Steve Jobs/Steve Wozniak relationship provides a powerful example when you're looking for business teammates: hold out for people who are on the same wavelength with you—people whose passions and focus are similar to your own.

Though Andy Grove and Steve Jobs shared a reputation for being difficult bosses, there was a big difference between them. For Steve, it was about the product and satisfying the customer. Andy's instructions and orders came across to me as power moves, very dictatorial. In fact, Intel had a policy called Creative Confrontation—which I saw as a way of providing a culture in which it was okay for Andy to chew people out!

The Role of the Team Leaders

A leader in the Steve Jobs model needs to have a set of lieutenants who can translate his goals and vision into detailed action plans. The success of Apple through the years has largely been due to Steve's talent for surrounding himself with people who could bear the heat when he wasn't satisfied, were strong enough to stand up to him when he was wrong, and were able to relay not just his instructions but his commitment, drive, and vision to the crew.

In an innovative organization, the role of the team leaders is more critical than in a traditional process-oriented organization. It's even more important in flat organizations where the leader is actively involved in the organization, operations, and key projects.

The key responsibilities of the team leaders are to balance the day-to-day operations and at the same time be the key advisors to the head honcho on the direction of the organization. They also have to be the liaison between the leader and the working-level troops—the designers, developers, engineers, and so on. Having the total ear of the leader and being a credible sounding board are key to the success of not just the team leaders but the company as a whole. Team leaders at Apple needed to be risk-takers and to have an entrepreneurial spirit.

Cross-Pollination and Monday Meetings

To keep the channels of communication open, Steve Jobs held a meeting with his lieutenants every Monday to go over the progress, review strategies, and address problems. These meetings were critical, a major tool for Steve to stay informed and in control of every aspect. But the value of the meetings went well beyond that: Steve stayed in touch constantly with every project—few things came up in the Monday meetings that he didn't already know about. He believed that all of his key people needed to know the status not just of his own projects but of all other projects, too. At the top level, he didn't believe in compartmentalizing: he held a strong conviction in a belief that might be called *cross-pollination*—a confidence that the best ideas and best solution to problems often come from someone working on a totally different project, perhaps with a widely different background and knowledge base.

When you have chosen your team leaders well, keep them informed about the status of every project, and ask for their ideas and input even on projects that aren't theirs.

Steve and the Use of Language

Steve's magic was working with the people of Apple to create artful products. When you are that deeply committed to your art, sometimes temperament plays a part in your behavior. Most people would find it a major accomplishment to do something life changing. But with Steve, it was ongoing, fired by an unmatchable intensity from the time he and Steve Wozniak started the company.

Steve brought his own personal language to his work, often communicating what he felt with just a word or two—just like the lyrics from the Beatles' songs "Let It Be" or "Hey Jude." At the same time, Steve seemed to lack the ability to understand the power he generated—probably the one area that I feel he could be criticized for. We all have a degree of power we need to take into account when dealing with people, whether employees, customers, or others.

From the early days of Apple, Steve never recognized his power, so the challenge was always figuring out what he meant. At any one moment, was he acting as the CEO, the visionary who was thinking way ahead of the market and products, or was he being forceful in pushing everyone to the next level?

Yet the language he used with the people around him was incredibly effective. But it was *his* language and you needed to understand it. He and I would have big fights—for example, over a product issue or something that was not happening as fast as he wanted—and he'd call me a "bozo."

It was one of his favorite terms when he was displeased, and it was unpleasant, but I was never offended. For Steve, it usually meant something like, "You need to get with my vision of the product." We all came to know it meant that he strongly disagreed with you. But it might also mean, "Tell me something to make me change my mind, or else shut up and stop wasting my time."

"Bozo" was on a par with that other favorite put-down of his—"That's shit"—most often addressed to a product engineer who was showing Steve his latest piece of work; it might mean, "That doesn't have the user interface I want." The engineers—at least, the ones not too thin skinned—came to understand that this also might mean, "I don't understand how that works" or "I don't understand why you designed it that way" And, "Explain it to me." Sometimes the explanation made the decision reasonable and valuable, after all, and Steve would go away satisfied—but never apologizing for his outburst; apologies were saved for family and the people closest to him.

The comment everybody around Steve longed to hear was "Insanely great." It was his highest praise and needs no explanation.

I think any leader has to be careful of how his or her language is interpreted. The persistence and charisma of Steve's style of communication were powerful tools. He could bring women to the point of tears but in an instant become quite charming. In the time I knew Steve, the person I saw cry the most was Steve himself. That was something few people ever saw and, again, not a trait we see in most leaders.

When in a conflict with Steve, I would envision, sitting there in front of me, all the users of the product that Apple would ever have, and having to deal with their criticism. Fixing the problem Steve was complaining about would save that barrage of complaints and criticisms; it was always worth the extra trouble of fixing the problem.

Dangers of the Middle Management Fear-of-Change Syndrome

In the traditional organization, there has always been a problem with the role of so-called middle managers. Do you know why Ford can't make a car as good as Volvo does? It goes back to back to the middle managers. Steve and I visited several car shows together, and we were always amazed at the so-called concept cars. The designs were magnificent, but we knew from experience that none of those cars would be turned into production models that customers could buy.

Why? Because the companies weren't following the lead of their head designers, their creators, their thinkers—people who were coming up with breakthrough technologies, only to be defeated by middle management.

Too often, middle managers are wage earners who see any change, however small, as a risk. Confidence lies in continuity, in continuing with what worked yesterday.

This was the culture I saw at IBM. Innovation there, it seemed to me, happened largely when the company acquired an outside firm that had developed some innovative new technology, or when IBM spun off a unit that was then able to function beyond the reach of the IBM corporate-think.

Within most large U.S. companies, innovation isn't impossible but usually requires such a struggle that the true innovators either leave or become plodders who have discovered that their best ideas are not likely to see the light of day and have just given up. Too often it's incredibly defeating to try to be innovative within the prison of a large company. This experience actually prompted me to write a letter to IBM Chairman Tom Watson Jr. and was one of the major reasons I left the company.

Lessons from a Mutiny

Though Steve was incredibly astute at interviewing and hiring people, he wasn't immune to mistakes, especially in those early Macintosh days when he was still honing his management skills.

When he was looking for someone to head up marketing for the Macintosh, Steve's eyes had lighted on Mike Murray, a bright MBA student who attended one of the roundtable seminars Steve was giving now and then at Stanford University, not far from the Apple campus. Mike had a diverse and impressive background. He had grown up in Oregon and had picked up early business experience from his family's creamery company. After getting an engineering degree from Stanford, he returned to Oregon and began working in the timber business for a time, then made an unlikely leap into the techno world by taking a job with Hewlett-Packard. That, in turn, led to a decision to get a business degree, which brought him back to Stanford.

Mike appeared to be a perfect match for Steve's small team. He had a million ideas for market approaches and programs for the Mac. At HP, he had worked on a project very similar to the Mac. Perhaps as a result, the marketing ideas he brought to Apple would turn out to be more suited to a traditional technology company like HP than to Apple.

His fundamental idea was to position and market the Macintosh, not to home users, but primarily as an appliance for *knowledge workers*—the term management guru Peter Drucker and others were using to describe what they envisioned as the corporate office workers of the future.

All the earlier members of the Mac team had dreamed of seeing the product of their handiwork in people's dens, living rooms, or even kitchens, and on desktops in students' dorm rooms. That's how the Mac would change society—by bringing computing power to the masses, to everyman, *not* by helping corporate employees work faster or more efficiently. Let someone else build those machines; that wasn't what the original Macintosh was all about.

This turned into a battle of conflicting visions waged on the high seas, with Captain Steve on one side, and Mike Murray on the other. Mike sought support for his view, and he found it in CEO John Sculley, whose reputation had been built on his marketing skills. John agreed with Mike that Apple should take on IBM, going after the corporate marketplace that IBM dominated.

Steve's resistance to this notion was part of his undoing, part of what led to his walking out of his own company and launching a rival firm. He was at that point in his life and career simply naïve about recognizing people who were willing to buy into his vision and move ahead with him at any risk.

After winning a battle he should have lost, Mike Murray followed Steve out the door, leaving Apple for a job at, of all places, Microsoft.

Steve's crucial error in the hiring of Mike Murray was his absolute conviction that Stanford was the best business training ground for anyone. What he failed to see was that the qualities of leadership needed for successful team leaders in an innovative, Pirate organization are the same qualities you need in a young company—qualities of entrepreneurship, risk-taking, and an absolute love of the product.

When Steve was selecting his Mac team leaders, he ignored these qualities and was blinded by the Stanford syndrome. Mike, with a background primarily shaped in corporate America, saw the MBA as a prelude to a job—a job not in a start-up company but in a mainstream corporation. Steve didn't yet know to be alert to the distinction. In the end, the mutiny of people like Mike turned to Steve's advantage.

In his years away from Apple, Steve grew much wiser about many things in business, including how to avoid choosing middle managers who hate taking risks and instead select loyal, entrepreneurial lieutenants who will thrive in a highly innovative organization.

Thinking of Everything

One of the most remarkable things about Steve Jobs is that he had his hand in every aspect of every project. *Every* aspect. When the Macintosh came out and wasn't doing very well, he decided he needed to find someone who could launch a Mac magazine that would offer the support Mac owners needed to address their concerns, keep them up with the latest developments, provide stories about new applications, and in the process, pique the interest and enthusiasm of people who were getting ready to buy a new computer and wanted some independent views on whether they should consider a Macintosh.

Steve saw the IBM PC, on the market three years ahead of the Mac, as the big competition. IBM was such a high-profile, highly respected company, carrying an aura of can-do-no-wrong, that its PC aimed at the consumer was looked on as the gold standard, even though the Mac was technologically superior by virtually every measure. There was already a magazine, *PC World*. Once Steve got the idea in his mind, nothing would do but find a way to launch a comparable magazine for the Mac.

I helped Steve in the search for a technology writer who had some knowledge of magazine publishing. The name that came up at the top of the list was David Bunnell. I set up an appointment and accompanied Steve, driving into San Francisco to meet with David.

Steve explained what he wanted and offered David a million dollars, with no strings and no voice in the content by Apple, if he would take on the project of creating and publishing a magazine on the Macintosh.

David struck me as a typical magazine editor—bright, very knowledge-able about the magazine industry. On the downside, he wasn't savvy about the Macintosh. Steve and I had a lively, encouraging interview with him, and it was clear David was eager to tackle a new challenge.

Steve asked me to step outside with him and asked what I thought. I told him I was impressed with the man's confidence and enthusiasm. Steve said, "Great, let's make it happen." We went back in. Steve announced, "It's a go," as he pulled a check out of his pocket and handed it over: a check for $1 million. (The board had given Steve signature authority for up to $10 million.)

I was shocked that he could do this so casually, but that was the power of being in charge.

As the new publisher, David brought in Andrew Fluegelman to become the editor, and they brought out the first issue before the end of 1984. They called the magazine *Macworld*, and it has been in publication ever since—currently published simultaneously in 10 countries, including Italy.

The Challenge of Finding New Team Leaders

When Apple Computer bought Steve's company NeXT, bringing Steve back into Apple, it was only months before Steve was put in charge as interim CEO, facing him with the incredible challenge of getting Apple back on course to become competitive again.

One of his first and most urgent tasks was to find the best possible team leaders to help him with the urgent rescue effort. How did he pick people he could rely on?

His choice for hardware engineering wasn't difficult. At NeXT, Steve had recruited Jon "Ruby" Rubinstein, whose impressive credentials included two degrees in electrical engineering from Cornell, a master's in computer science, experience working for Hewlett-Packard, plus design work on supercomputers at another company. When Apple purchased NeXT, Steve recommended Ruby to the then-CEO, Gil Amelio.

With Apple floundering and many outside observers pronouncing that the company might not survive, many people would have turned the job down—anybody would think twice about signing on with a company that might go under at any time. Ruby later explained, "Apple was the last innovative high-volume computer maker in the world."[1] He accepted the challenge.

Since Steve had always put more emphasis than almost anyone else in the business world on the external appearance of the products, it wasn't a surprise that he would look for first-class design talent. Great product design would be a key element for getting the Apple products selling again.

Steve typically is given most of the credit for the great design of Apple products. He deserves credit for being so demanding and for setting such high standards, but he also deserves credit for recognizing the ability of a talent already at Apple but thinking of jumping ship. Jonathon "Jony" Ive, a Brit who was head of the company's design team, had been suffering from a familiar problem: nobody at Apple had been paying the kind of attention to design that Steve had always thought was such a critical element.

When Steve made it clear his goal was not to produce big profits but to make great products, that was all the encouragement Jony needed to stay.

Still, the connection almost didn't work out. Steve had begun a search for a new chief of design, talking to people who had created products he greatly admired, including Italian Giorgetto Giugiaro, who early in his career had stunned car enthusiasts with his very first major design, the 1967 Maserati Ghibli—still considered one of the stellar examples that inspired the era of exotic supercars. Steve, as you might know, had always had a special love for well-designed cars.

One day while still searching, Steve wandered into Apple's design studio. He could tell from the models and sketches that this was a workshop of people who understood the word *elegant*. And he could tell from his conversation with Jony that Apple already had a design chief who shared his sensibility about the importance of design. By the end of that first conversation, Steve recognized that he could forget about his search for a new design chief, and Jony was convinced he would be staying at Apple.

It was clear they shared the same passion for great design. What was also clear was that Jony totally bought into Steve's vision for Apple and was fully willing to accept the difficulties of working under the pressure of Apple's resurgent leader.

For me, the great lesson in this story lies in knowing your own values so well that you can instinctively recognize someone who shares those values. Jony was close to leaving Apple, and Steve was so close to bringing in an outside designer. Instead, their great connection that day would prove to be a major factor in making the iPod, iPhone, and iPad products that set an entirely new standard in every aspect of their design.

A few months after connecting with Jony, Steve made his next major addition of another key lieutenant—one who would come to have an especially great impact on the company. Apple's head of operations had buckled under the pressure of working for Steve and quit. Steve took over the duties himself, while looking for a replacement. The search proved tougher than he expected, since he wanted someone who had mastered just-in-time manufacturing, like the factories Steve had created for the Mac and for the NeXT computers. He searched for a year before finding Tim Cook, who had a degree in industrial engineering, a master's in business, and experience working at IBM. One major difficulty: Tim had recently taken a job at Compaq Computers. In a phrase Cook would repeat frequently through the years, he said that five minutes into his job interview with Steve, "I wanted to throw caution and logic to the wind and join Apple."

It would involve throwing caution and logic to the wind because everyone in the industry had heard stories of Steve's reputation for making great demands on his employees, at times treating even his closest lieutenants harshly.

Tim Cook's skills as a manager combined with his desire to make the best products possible qualified him as the kind of lieutenant that Steve had been looking for. He differed from Steve in personality; the often-repeated phrase labels him "mild-mannered and diligent." Still, it's widely agreed that they had one thing in common: competitiveness.

Today as CEO, Tim Cook, like Steve before him, is in business to create great, enduring products—salary and perks are not the focus. What Steve saw in Tim was his ability to handle major corporate strategic decisions, combined with the ability to operate in a start-up environment, with a flat organization, and be a partner to a strong leader. He was really an entrepreneur at heart but had the big-company wisdom to be able to handle the Apple environment. And he could handle Steve.

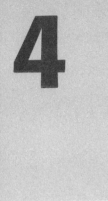

Steve's Secrets for Selecting Great People

A small team of A-players can run circles around a giant team of B- and C-players.

—Steve Jobs[1]

Hiring decisions present one of the key challenges to creating a Pirate culture. As Steve put it, key hiring decisions are as important as creating a new product. He even put a good hire on the same level as the moment he first saw a graphical user interface and a mouse, at the Xerox Palo Alto Research Center, and realized they would be the cornerstones for the future of computing. So many companies have a culture that encourages people to fall into line, just like life in The Navy. These types of organizations generally are able to accomplish little more than improving on the innovative ideas of others.

Too often we hire clones—worthy clones, hardworking, ambitious, disciplined, compliant, well educated, often trained and proven in a competitive firm. You know the story. Just look around you, maybe even at yourself.

To really succeed in a fast-changing world where yesterday's rules are being broken every day, we need to learn to be brave and resist the usual, the familiar.

As advertising guru David Ogilvy wrote in his book *Confessions of an Advertising Man*, "Business needs massive transfusions of talent. And talent, I believe, is most likely to be found among non-conformists, dissenters and rebels."[2]

Miles Young, the global CEO of Ogilvy & Mather, has recommended that business people "hire more nutters." One night over a cocktail at the Zeta Bar in Sydney, I asked him, "Is a nutter the same as a Pirate?"

"No," he said. "They're different. But they serve the same purpose. Nutters think totally differently than us. They come at things from a very different perspective. Pirates are on the same wavelength, but do it their own way and with their rules."

Positive deviants is another term I've heard to describe this type. And former British prime minister Tony Blair, in his autobiography, described them as crazy people. "In my experience," he wrote, "there are two types of crazy people: those who are just crazy, and therefore dangerous; and those whose craziness lends them creativity, strength, and ingenuity, and verve."[3]

I *love* these ideas. You want people who dare to be different! You want Pirates—where the skull and crossbones may not be part of the company's symbol, but they're Pirates nonetheless. People who take risks, live at times a little on the edge, flaunt rules when justified, laugh loudly as the wind lashes their face and their pursuers fade from view into the distance behind. I always want to work with people like this, and so should you.

Whether you think of them as nonconformists, dissenters, rebels, pirates, nutters, positive deviants, or as Blair's crazies, make sure your team has a solid sprinkling of them. They will challenge your thinking, fuel your ideas, pump up your momentum, boost your competitive edge, and quite simply make your business a winner.

And make sure you yourself provide a dose of this magic on occasion. You're unlikely to accomplish anything great in your career without it.

Wisdom Required

Steve had this almost scary view of the culture he wanted, the kinds of people who were suited to that culture, and the mix of people required to round out the needs. It was as if he had simply grasped intuitively the ultimate landscape necessary to build and sell the ultimate product.

Yet when Steve first organized the Mac group and selected its leaders, he was so caught up in having young, entrepreneurial people that he missed one crucial factor: the need for *wisdom*. Life experiences have a major importance in determining if you are up to the responsibility being placed on your shoulders, especially in terms of handling major problems and major disappointments.

He soon recognized the need to include what he had taken to calling *people of wisdom*. By that he meant people like me—a good deal older than 22 (which if I recall was, incredibly, the average age of the techies on the original Mac team). And not just older, but with the kind of real-world business knowledge only acquired from the experience of working your way through tough challenges of product development, meeting marketplace demands, and finding ways to cope with the often unrealistic corporate restrictions of how-it's-always-done-around-here.

Your First Ten People

For their book *In the Company of Giants*, authors Rama Dev Jager and Rafael Ortiz, interviewing Steve, asked him about putting together a team. He told them that "in most things in life, the dynamic range between average quality and the best quality is, at most, two-to-one." But in advanced fields—he used the example of hardware design—he observed that "the dynamic range between what an average person could accomplish and what the best person could accomplish was 50 or 100 to 1."

When Jager and Ortiz challenged Steve by pointing out that a manager, especially in a start-up, may not have much time to spend hunting for talent and interviewing candidates, Steve came down heavily: "I disagree totally," he said. "I think it's the *most important* job."

He told them, "When you're in a startup, the first ten people will determine whether the company succeeds or not."

His conclusion was that you must find extraordinary people: "the cream of the cream."[4]

Project Groups

Steve believed in small, integrated units. He had a vision of a project group always small enough that every member—*every* member—stayed involved all the way through. Off-site meetings for the entire team were one key way of making that happen. The commitments made at a meeting in front of all team members were sometimes even more powerful than a one-on-one promise to Steve; they were essential for keeping projects on schedule.

For me, the timing of the first Macintosh off-site was perfect, coming not long after I joined Apple. Though I had been hired to be vice president of human resources for the entire company, Steve also included me as a member of the Mac team. So I had two jobs: one on the corporate side with responsibilities for the whole company, the other as a kind of graybeard for Steve—older, more experienced in business, and with my years at IBM and Intel, more experienced as well in the world of technology.

A Process for Hiring

Want to recruit and hire highly talented innovators? Here are some Jobsian ideas for hiring:

1. Define the requirements, but don't be rigid.

   At first glance, this point will sound painfully obvious. But in my experience, too often the person doing the hiring has not given enough thought to defining the need precisely enough. When that's the case, you might be interviewing the perfect person and not realize it. Or the person in charge of filling the position might be looking for the wrong type of candidate. Worse, you run a high risk of hiring the wrong person—guaranteed to set your project back.

   Steve always had a very clear grasp of the need. Yet at the same time, he was not at all rigid about what qualifications he was looking for. Sometimes his choices surprised me, when he saw something in a candidate hardly anyone else would have seen—something that told him, "This is the right person for the job."

   That's what happened with Susan Kare. At her high school in Pennsylvania, Susan had known a guy who would become one of the early Mac team members, Andy Hertzfeld, and the two had kept in touch.

   Steve was captivated by the "graphical user interface" he had seen at Xerox's Palo Alto Research Center, which used icons on the screen to make routine operations obvious and easy; you use such an icon every time you drag something to the trashcan symbol to let the computer know you want to delete that item.

Who was going to dream up those icons, and the other parts of a pleasing and easy-to-use onscreen design? Andy suggested Susan, whom he knew had become an accomplished artist. Almost any other executive in those circumstances would not have agreed to let Susan come in for an interview: she was a creative artist who knew nothing about technology. She had *not qualified* written all over her.

But Steve saw in her a spark, the ability to catch on quickly, and the kind of creativity that suggested she wouldn't be locked into old concepts but would be able to offer the kind of inventive contributions Steve was committed to having. He decided that Susan's talent, passion, and flair were more important than the fact that her background in technology was a big blank. He accepted her as a key part of the Mac team.

It turned out to be an inspired choice and another example of Steve's ability to judge a person by more than their résumé.

And that, as well, is how she came to be around when the Macintosh Pirate flag needed the hand of an artist.

2. Make the team part of the hiring process.

Steve intuitively understood the importance of making the whole team part of the process. That was a priority, probably *the* main priority, of the frequent off-site meetings at ocean-side resorts on Monterey Bay, about an hour's drive from Cupertino.

In addition to team members reporting on their progress and the challenges they faced, these off-sites were also an opportunity for speaking up when you discovered you could not keep on schedule without adding another person to your group, or when you were going to be facing the need for some special talent that nobody on the current Mac team possessed.

The same was true for the weekly team meetings. Part of the discussion about the progress of the individual Mac teams involved what positions needed to be filled and what talent we had to recruit. Steve always believed that what he always called A-players were most likely hanging around with other A-players and so were themselves the most likely source for suggesting people for the team.

The idea of asking your people to collar any friend or acquaintance they think might be suitable to fill an opening has carried over to the Apple stores.

3. Don't limit your search to the usual methods.

Even under the intense pressure of bringing the Macintosh to life, Steve's accepting invitations to lecture to classes at Stanford University became part of his routine, and he often asked me to keep him company. Even without any preparation I was ever aware of, he was always fascinating at those sessions. The students considered it a rare privilege to be able to discuss real-life business problems with an entrepreneur whose start-up company was already in the forefront of the new industry of personal computers, and his face was more familiar than anyone else in the computer industry. For Steve, these visits were rewarding because, though a college dropout, he had a deep respect for the benefits of education.

But it was a two-way street. Steve was so good at those sessions because he felt inspired and energized by the students. And as always, everywhere he went, he always had his antennae up to find likely candidates for the Macintosh group.

Mike Murray was a 20-something MBA student at one of the sessions Steve addressed. Mike said that he and others at the class at first thought Steve was a student since he brought nothing with him—no briefcase, no presentation equipment, no notes. But when he started talking, Steve spoke plainly about Apple and how we were trying to change the world with personal computers. That was all Mike needed to hear; he wanted to be part of it. Steve was impressed, and Mike was given the job of heading up the marketing group for the Mac.

Bob Bellville was 21 in the spring of 1981 and just about to graduate from Stanford. For some eight years he had been working at least part time (and full time during some summers) at Xerox PARC in their Learning Research Group. Steve saw that Bob had a deep insight into how to build technology into a total product. He understood the parts of the Xerox PARC technology that Steve was using, and he had a background to oversee the building of the Mac. Bob also had valuable insight into how a company should operate, which Steve liked. He saw a very smart engineer who had independent thought and technical leadership abilities. Recruiting Bob wasn't a challenge.

Someone at Stanford gave Steve the name of Mike Boich, a former Stanford undergrad who had gone on to earn an MBA at Harvard.

Steve got in touch with Mike and hired him. He proved to be another good choice. It was Mike Boich who tackled one of the toughest challenges facing the Macintosh when it was launched, coining the word *evangelists* for people on the team he helped assemble: their job was to persuade software developers to create software programs for the Mac, and it proved to be a very successful effort—so crucial that the Macintosh might not have survived without the evangelists.

Incidentally, Steve found more than an assortment of hard-charging new employees at Stanford. He also found the young woman he would marry, Laurene Powell.

Talented People Know Other Talented People

It's become part of the history of Silicon Valley that Steve often said, "Make sure you're hiring only A-players." Hire a few B-players, he said, and they hire Bs and Cs, and pretty soon the whole operation is going to pot.

Obviously not everyone can afford to hire only A-players. So how do you find people who are exceptionally talented and a good fit for the team?

As mentioned earlier, one of the greatest sources of talented prospects is your own employees. Really sharp people generally prefer the company of other really sharp people. When you need to hire someone, you ask the people on the team to recommend somebody they admire.

Steve said employees who did this should be given a reward for helping the company in its recruiting efforts. So he and I set up a program called Esprit de Corps, which paid employees $500 for every new hire they had recommended. We also gave each a lapel button like one awarded to World War I pilots for doing a great job in the air battles, along with a T-shirt stating they had just been awarded the badge. It was more hype than real, but it worked—reminding and encouraging others to think about A-players they could recommend.

The team member who brought the person in was held accountable to make sure the new hire had all the information needed to be successful, so the relationship was ongoing.

Eventually the new Macintosh employees' reward program came to be used all over Apple.

Making your best talent central to the recruiting process is a secret to sustaining creativity. Many of the people brought in as the group expanded were suggested by team members. A classic example was Chris Espinosa, who when he was a college freshman had as his advisor a man named Andy Hertzfeld. Andy became one of the early Mac Pirates; when the need came up for someone to create a Macintosh owner's manual, Andy suggested Chris. How well did it work out? Chris was employee number eight and is *still* at Apple as I write this.

An Updated Version

Today, the tactic of paying employees for finding new talent is widespread. A San Francisco company called Practice Fusion offers an example of this approach at work. The company helps people put their medical information online in a way that is secure yet makes the information readily available to any hospital or doctor when needed. When a candidate is hired, the company rewards the employee who introduced the person with a payment that can be as high as $10,000. Maybe that's part of the reason Practice Fusion is the largest and fastest growing in its field.

Journalist Sharlyn Lauby tells a story she heard from an employee of a small young company providing services in its local area. "Two years ago," the employee had told her, "one of our CEO's friends introduced us to an engineer from a big tech company. We didn't think much of it—he was happy with his job, and we weren't looking to hire anyone."

But something about the atmosphere at the company had obviously appealed to the man. "He started coming to our offices on Friday nights to hang out with the team." They realized later that the man had kept coming because he had been picking up clues about the pulse of the company. "He saw over time how . . . excited we were about our progress, how rapidly we improved our product, how big our dreams were." Soon he "caught the startup bug."

The ending of the story goes even beyond what you might expect. "Skip ahead two years to today. He's now our lead engineer." He even brought along his roommate—"another big-tech-firm engineer"—who also joined the start-up team.[5]

And then there was the case of a San Francisco company with the odd name of I Love Rewards. They were throwing twice-a-month cocktail parties at the upscale W Hotel for their employees and executives. The functions had a dual purpose: they built camaraderie and team spirit, but they also provided the company with an opportunity to give job candidates the chance to meet staffers in a much less intimidating environment than a formal job interview. In the relaxed, laid-back setting of the hotel, staffers were able to size up candidates, while the candidates soaked up a sense of positive vibes of the company's people. It was a chance for both sides to talk about goals and expectations.

As of this writing, I Love Rewards—now bearing the more gracious company name of Achievers—was expanding so fast that their website carried an announcement of their "biggest recruiting effort in company history."

Choosing People Who Can Adapt to the Style of the Leader

In time, I learned a lesson about dealing with Steve when he was harsh, angry, or abusive over a decision or suggestion made or some work presented. My insight came through the experience of an executive on the Mac team. To protect his reputation, I'll call him Don Vincent.

Steve was looking for someone to lead the creation of the multimillion-dollar Mac factory, and the search led to Don, who was then working at Hewlett-Packard and had a lot of solid recommendations. Once Don started working for Apple, it became clear he was not really an entrepreneur at heart and, even worse, he had a very thin skin—not a good quality in someone working for Steve Jobs.

For example, on one meeting where Don was making a presentation about the factory robots, Steve was very unhappy with the selections Don was presenting. He bounded out of his chair and started waving his hands like a robot, carrying on in something of a frenzy. At one point he demanded, "Don, if you were a robot, what color would you want to be!?"

No one in the history of manufacturing had ever been asked to deal with the feelings of a robot! Don was dumbfounded by the question and very embarrassed in front of the staff. He had no response to offer. Instead of pushing back, he took the criticism personally. He got up and left the room.

After the meeting, I told Steve, "You need to be careful in how you talk to a sensitive person like Don, particularly putting him down in front of the group." I also told him, "It's okay to attack me, because I understand you, and I can accept it. But Don took it very personally. You need to meet with him and apologize and make sure he understands what you were trying to communicate—that it was not personal."

Before Steve could meet with him, Don had found himself another job and handed in his resignation. I couldn't get him to change his mind. When I told Steve, his reaction was that Don "isn't a Pirate." But at our next Monday meeting with the staff, Steve led me to bring up a discussion about the incident, which we discussed as a mistake, one that we hopefully learned from.

This is a lesson that applies with all strong-willed leaders: When there's a blowup, don't let it go without closure on the issues. And another lesson: In the hiring process, we were so wrapped up in issues of Don's ability to build the factory that we missed the key element of "could he deal with the Pirate leader?" In Don's previous job at Hewlett-Packard, the culture of "the HP Way" was very easy going, with not much criticism ever given to anyone. This was the experience that taught Steve and me that not everyone can adapt to a Pirate culture. Nor can everyone adapt to a leader who is at times as harsh and critical as Steve.

Special Hiring: Another Example

Today when you walk into an Apple store, every experience—from the welcome greetings to customers, to things running on the demo computers, iPods, iPads, and iPhones—is carefully planned. Today's Apple sales training is about dealing with customers instead of closing sales. The Apple training manual is about steps to service, laid out in an acronym APPLE, where A stands for Approach, and so on.

Employees are trained to avoid telling a customer, "I don't understand." If a customer mispronounces a product name, employees are taught not to correct the person. Employees at Apple's retail stores are expected to understand the issues of their clients and make an extra effort to find solutions for them.

No wonder Apple stores generate more visitors per quarter than Disney's top four amusement parks together see in a year. The Apple stores' annual sales per square foot, as of 2011, is over $5,600, far ahead of all other U.S. chains. Second place goes to the exclusive, up-scale jewelry chain of Tiffany & Co, in business for well over a century; for Tiffany, the comparable sales figure is less than $3,000 per square foot. What's more, the total annual sales of the Apple stores increased in 2011 by a nearly unbelievable 70 percent over the previous year; the comparable figure for Tiffany was 15 percent.

Clearly, the training of the staff in the Apple stores has paid off.

The late, great American anthropologist, Margaret Mead once said, "Never doubt that a small group of thoughtful, committed citizens can change the world. Indeed, it is the only thing that ever has."

5 Unusual Interviewing Techniques

Here's to the crazy ones, the misfits, the rebels, the troublemakers, the round pegs in the square holes . . . because the ones who are crazy enough to think that they can change the world, are the ones who do.

—Apple Ad

Recruiting should never be an effort just of the human resources people. Hiring should be a collaborative process, and it should be based on a culture that is focused on finding the A-players. A candidate should speak with at least a dozen people in several areas of the company, not just those in the area that he or she would work in. That way your prospective A-employees get broad exposure to the needs and activities of other parts of the company.

Steve completely revised my ideas on the subject of job interviews. My understanding of what he was doing began when I thought back over our first conversation in the restaurant that shifted into a Steve Jobs version of an employment interview. I call it a Steve Jobs version because he had a unique way of interviewing that was less of an interview and more of a conversation. Instead I was getting my first taste of his highly personal interviewing style, which I would come to recognize as a basic underlying element—possibly *the* most important element—in assembling the teams that through the years enabled him to turn out that incredible stream of phenomenal, paradigm-changing, gotta-have products.

Once I became an Apple employee, Steve often asked me, as VP of human resources, to have a conversation with candidates after they had finished talking to him. Many of those people told me that their session with Steve hadn't seemed like an interview. No wonder. They have been served up a taste of the Steve Jobs non-interview.

So you have a promising candidate coming in. How are you going to conduct the interview? Here are some pointers of the Steve Jobs technique.

Résumé? Don't Bother

First of all, he was never much interested in a person's résumé. A résumé only speaks to what the person has achieved in the past. Instead, Steve most of all wanted to know about the candidates, *What can they bring to this project? What is the talent they bring? What do I see that says they can go beyond?*

"Let Me Tell You Where We're Going"

One of the challenges was that Steve, as you very likely know, was inordinately secretive about Apple's projects. He might be looking for someone who would be able to, say, solve some thorny problems about the antenna for a proposed cell phone that no one even guessed Apple might be working on. He might say something like, "Let me tell you where we're trying to go," or "Let me show you something I'm thinking about," and pull out something as seemingly unimportant as a piece of plastic with a new color on it. He was always very interested in the getting other people's reaction to physical design.

Or it might be, "What do you think of the design of my watch?" I always knew that if the applicant left with a new watch like Steve's, it meant the person had recognized the beauty of the design, and Steve had rewarded his good taste by reaching into the box in his desk and presenting the person with a duplicate of his own as a gift. Those watches cost something like $2,000, but Steve gave duplicates away to anyone who recognized the excellence of the design.

Leaving the Door Open

Steve wouldn't *ask* if you had some ideas that might be of value or some crucial talents that might be helpful. He would just leave the door open to see if you came forth with anything that made sense. That's why people came away feeling they had had a conversation with him instead of having been interviewed: He didn't ask, "What can you do for me?" He just gave people the opportunity to speak up, so he could judge whether it sounded as if they could offer a contribution to the project and the team.

The unspoken questions were, "What is the talent you bring?" and "What do I see that says you can go beyond and become a valuable contributor, an innovator?"

I met a man years later who had been interviewed by Steve, who complained to me at the time about the way he had been treated. It turned out that he had gotten off on the wrong foot right from the start by showing up in a three-piece business suit—revealing at a glance that he hadn't taken the trouble to find out anything about the Apple culture. Then the man wanted to show Steve a piece of work he was proud of, which he had brought with him on his computer. He reached into his briefcase and pulled out a Dell laptop. The interview was over the instant Steve saw the Dell.

Will This Person Be Able to Share Bad News?

One other element about Steve's conversations with job candidates: he wanted to get a sense of whether the person would be honest with him. As he explained to me once, "If there's bad news, will they have the guts to tell me, or will they try to hide it?"

"Have You Ever Been Fired?"

In that first restaurant conversation, Steve asked a question that is definitely not the kind of thing people who observe the ordinary social graces would ever ask a complete stranger: "Jay, have you ever been fired?"

I laughed. "No," I said. "But I once anticipated being fired and quit to avoid it. I had been hired by a radio station as a disc jockey, and it wasn't a very good match for my talents, clearly not what the station was looking for. It didn't take a genius to figure out that they weren't going to keep me around, so I walked into the owner's office and told him I was quitting. He said, 'Thanks. You just saved yourself from being fired!' "

Steve got a kick out of the story. I would discover later that he didn't really care whether a person he was interviewing had ever been fired. He asked the question because he wanted to see the reaction: Would the person be embarrassed? Caught off guard? Stumped about whether or not to tell the truth? The reaction told him a lot more about candidates than what they actually said.

Looking for a Reaction

Candidates who survived those early parts of the interview with Steve then got the Steve Jobs sales pitch. He would lay out his vision with such enthusiasm and passion that it would be hard to say no.

When he could do it without compromising secrecy, he would sometimes show a prototype of some component that didn't give anything away. On one occasion, after he had left Apple and started NeXT Computers, he was talking to an Apple employee he wanted to recruit for NeXT. He waxed poetic about this groundbreaking personal computer he and his teams were designing—and then showed off one state-of-the-art item. In fact, it was nothing more than a length of cable, but it was a cable that had been designed especially for the NeXT, to Steve's very demanding standard. He displayed it with the reverence and awe that someone else might have lavished on a Rembrandt painting. Still, that innocuous cable was as much of the computer as Steve was willing to show, even to this trusted Apple employee he knew personally and was so eager to recruit.

Why bother showing something as essentially insignificant as a piece of cable? Because, again, he was looking for the reaction.

If I had been asked, "How should I let Mr. Jobs know I really want to work for him?" I would have answered, "Don't mask your enthusiasm. If you see or hear something that gets you excited, *let him see it*."

I've followed that principle in my own interviewing ever since, often hiring people who would not have passed muster based on their résumés but who turned out to be brilliant choices. The trick is to give people the opportunity to show what they care about, what excites them. Remember, sometimes it's not what they say but how they react that is the critical element in deciding whether you want them on your team.

Judging the Ability to Contribute

In my case, once I had agreed to take the job at Apple, Steve laid out two tests for me. One involved the Apple II computer he had sent to me. It was a good thing I was curious enough to sit right down and learn how to use it. The day I arrived, he already expected me to be proficient.

The other test was the visit to Xerox PARC I described in my previous book. He didn't tell me where we were headed but as he drove us there, with the music blaring, he asked what I thought of the Apple II and where I thought computers were going.

Again he was giving himself an opportunity to judge my reaction. He wanted to find out whether I shared his worldview about computers. I told him I found the Apple II exciting but that I was sure future machines could be made much easier to learn and to use.

This part of the probing had actually begun in our original conversation, and I would come to recognize it as a standard part of his routine with job candidates. "How do you like the Apple products?" he had asked. Since I had never seen an Apple product, much less used one, I told him I had to answer based on what I had seen—some IBM products in the development lab, the PC prototype Intel was working on, and the Osborne computer I had used at Intel. My experience was limited but, I told him, it seemed you almost had to be a programmer to use the products. The user interface was very technical. In addition, most people (back then) had a fear of computers. The word itself, based on IBM's positioning of the computer market, brought a sense of remote awe and discomfort. I said, "If people had felt that way about the telephone, we'd still be communicating by mail." Steve smiled in appreciation.

He had opened the door with his question. I had given him just the kind of reaction he was looking for.

The Below-Decks Crew Members

For some positions, you need people with spirit, yet the job is the equivalent of working in the galley. A prime example: hiring people to work in the Apple retail stores.

Working in an Apple store is a coveted position, more sought after than you might imagine: Only about 6 percent of the applicants are chosen. Candidates frequently try to find out how to prepare themselves so they can ace the personal interview. In fact, it's not something a person can prepare for, because it's about attitude, work ethic, and being a team player. And, as well, having passion for the products, having a collaborative spirit, and paying great attention to details. The recruiting process Apple uses is completely different from a job at the company headquarters in Cupertino. Some applicants have been interviewed on a bench in the mall, in a coffee shop, or at an outdoor restaurant.

Another company that has also done a great job of recruiting people to fit their culture is Starbucks. As they grew, the headquarters staff increased from 100 employees to 1,000. On the front lines, they were faced with even a bigger challenge: how to hire over 100,000 new employees without losing their existing culture, which has always been based on the people behind the counter being able to make a connection with the customer. Starbucks senior vice president Dave Olson described their culture by saying that it didn't matter how many millions or billions of coffees the company served, if a single customer received one that didn't suit him/her, the staff had to be able to perform automatically to address it and make sure the customer was satisfied.

On Not Using Recruiters

Steve believed from the first that you could not rely on outside recruiting firms to select people who would be a good fit for the Apple culture.

Talking to *Fortune* senior editor Betsy Morris in 2008, Steve told her that rather than using outside search firms, Apple did its own talent searching. "Recruiting is hard," he told her. "It's just finding the needles in the haystack. We do it ourselves and we spend a lot of time at it."

For Steve, this wasn't just a now-and-then task that he found time for when things were slow. "I've participated in the hiring of maybe 5,000-plus people in my life—so I take it very seriously. You can't know enough in a one-hour interview."

It's the talent of sizing up whether the person is a truly good fit for the culture that Steve developed and nurtured. "In the end," he said in the *Fortune* interview, "it's ultimately based on your gut. 'How do I feel about this person? What are they like when they're challenged? Why are they here?' I ask everybody that: 'Why are you here?'"

He finished with a statement that sums up the essence of what I think of as the Steve Jobs culture standard: "The answers themselves are not what you're looking for. It's the meta-data"—by which he meant the information you draw from the data.[1]

All Hands on Deck

In the end, the most important element in creating a Pirate organization is choosing the right people, and the most important element in choosing the right people is being able to recognize the values and qualities of Pirates when you see them.

That means you have to know who you are as an organization, you have to have a clear product vision, and you have to have a clear sense of the culture you're trying to create. Steve was describing the culture of innovation when he said that "Apple runs like a start-up." He meant that the company has small teams of Pirates working with a tight focus on one important project at a time.

I once asked an old Apple friend what he missed most about Apple after he left. He answered, "A CEO and executive team with great vision and a great ability to communicate direction that ripples down through the company." That's as good a definition as any of the Pirate organization.

6

To Protect Innovation, Create a Company within a Company

[I]t's building an environment that makes people feel they are surrounded by equally talented people and their work is bigger than they are. The feeling that the work will have tremendous influence and is part of a strong, clear vision.

—Steve Jobs[1]

You can't throw a stone in Silicon Valley without hitting a start-up, and the same is nearly as true today in New York, Boston, and Austin, Barcelona, Berlin, and Tel Aviv. But the picture is completely different when trying to launch an innovative start-up *within* an established, traditional company.

In cases like this, the way that you organize is as critical as the people you choose for your organization or the products or services you deliver. Steve Jobs became an icon in part for what he achieved by going against the tide of traditional wisdom about how to run a company. He wasn't the first to create a stand-alone development group within a larger corporation, but his Macintosh group became the prototype for how to make it happen and how to make it work successfully.

I witnessed that the very week I started at Apple. At Steve's invitation, on a cloudy Saturday in February 1981, I joined him for a drive to a destination he had carefully avoided naming. It turned out to be a destination featured in every history of Apple. We were headed for the Xerox Corporation's super-secret Palo Alto Research Center, better known as Xerox PARC. On the way over, Steve told me about PARC, describing it as a kingdom of PhD nerds who "didn't get it." But he thought there was some great talent there we could use. So one of my assignments for the visit was to get contact info from some of the talented people we met and follow up with them later.

The building itself was nothing special, giving no hint of the advanced technology being developed inside those walls. Most of the people we met were very guarded and not very friendly. I found out later that most of them did not know that Xerox was a major investor. Despite their caution, they totally underestimated Steve's ability to absorb their technology.

As you may know, it was on this and two earlier visits that Steve picked up the ideas for making the Macintosh so unique and setting Apple on its course to success. (I have sometimes wondered what would have become of Apple if Xerox had said no to Steve's request to visit.)

On the way back, Steve had a laser-like stare that I eventually understood as his "I have a vision and the plan to make it happen" look. I was to experience this look many times.

By the time Steve came to work the Monday morning after our PARC visit, he already knew what the product was he wanted to develop and how it would work. It was only a matter of figuring out how to go about it.

Taking Over

When I joined Apple, a remarkable man, Jef Raskin, had until recently been leading a small team of people working on developing a next-generation breakthrough product for Apple. Jef had a fascinating background. He had won a national award from the American Rocket Society when most kids his age were still learning algebra. By the time he joined Apple, he had degrees in mathematics and physics (with minors in philosophy and music), and he had held positions as an associate professor of music, assistant professor of visual arts, and even as an assistant instructor of bicycling. He had written and scored the music for a show on PBS, conducted the San Francisco Chamber Opera Company, and had a one-man show of his paintings at the Los Angeles County Museum of Art.

Jef met the two Steves when they were introducing the Apple II at the first West Coast Computer Faire and was hired soon after. Though it was well outside his area of responsibilities (he was in charge of documentation), he wrote a stream of memos about how to make the computer into a truly convenient device. He put those ideas into motion by finagling permission to assemble a small development team to build a new kind of personal computer.

Steve tried to convince Jef that the graphical user interface and the mouse in use at Xerox PARC would become the new face of computing. Jef was just as convinced that what Steve wanted would make the machine too expensive for the masses.

Though cofounder of Apple, Steve Jobs was now in career limbo, with no specific duties or responsibilities, no project he was in charge of. Meanwhile, Apple management was in disarray, with entrepreneur Mike Scott still CEO and investor Mike Markkula still board chairman. I joined Apple because of Steve's dynamic personality, his intensity, and his almost mystical degree of enthusiasm—but the CEO and chairman totally failed to recognize this. It has sometimes seemed to me that I was the only person in leadership at Apple back then who recognized these qualities; Steve sensed this, and it was one of the key reasons that he and I became so close, along with his seeing me as a mentor because of my years of experience working for IBM and Intel.

Scotty and Mike saw Steve's brashness as a red flag. But when he said he wanted to take over Jef Raskin's small development team, they gave him carte blanche, removing Jef from leadership of the team he had created and handing the reins over to Steve. They did this not because they were convinced Steve was going to be able to create a great product, but to get him out of their hair. He had been a nuisance, showing up in the work area of the Lisa, which management looked on as the company's next-generation computer, and haranguing the engineers about what they were doing wrong. They had little understanding of what he was going on about—a mouse, icons, pull-down menus, and the like—and thought he was just being a distraction and annoyance. They wanted to get him out of the way.

It's not hard to understand. People of vision have a hard time in traditional companies. They want to throw off the chains and charge ahead, and that just doesn't go down well in any conventional business.

As for Jef, he was able to build his machine—but only after he left Apple and joined another company that was willing to let him do it his way. He was a brilliant man, highly accomplished, with skills outshining many of the leading talents in half a dozen fields, but his computer flopped.

Steve—driven, driving, never easy to work for—had developed an instinct for what would best serve the average consumer. Now having taken over Jef's team, he was able to lead the development of their computer according to his own personal vision.

There was one carryover from Jef: he had already named the computer "Macintosh."

Reviving a Radical Idea: A Virtual Company within a Company

Steve created what would become a company within Apple, a virtual company that for all practical purposes had almost nothing to do with the rest of Apple.

In our daily conversations (my office was only 20 feet from his) and on our frequent walks outside, around the buildings, Steve talked often about his frustration that Apple was quickly turning into a company with a traditional structure and way of operating. He talked a lot about the danger, often speaking of the rest of Apple and especially the other product groups as "the bozo organizations." They were hiring people with the right degrees and the right experience at other companies, paying little attention to whether they had the start-up mentality.

He didn't want the Mac group to be dragged into this and lose the entrepreneurial focus—the ability to see and be motivated by an inspiring vision of the future.

He went to his original partner, Steve Wozniak, who had been responsible for creating the original Apple computer and the Apple II, and for choosing the hardware engineers and programmers. Steve told Woz, "We need to build a new team for the Macintosh." Woz fully bought into that, but his heart still belonged to the Apple II, which was his own creation. Before Jobs could get any support from his start-up partner, Woz crashed an airplane he was flying—stalling on takeoff in a type of plane he wasn't sufficiently familiar with. He was seriously injured, even losing some of his memory for a time, and wasn't around to give Steve Jobs the support he longed for.

It was clear to Steve that he needed to make Macintosh a start-up organization, totally separated from the rest of Apple. In fact, he and I later talked about Macintosh being spun out as a separate company, to be called Macintosh Corporation—still owned mostly if not entirely by Apple, but run independently by Steve. I went to the board to make the case for this, pointing out that Steve had created this separate organization that was essentially independent of Apple and that it would be far better for Apple as well as for Macintosh to give him total authority for running it. As far as I could tell, the board never even gave the idea serious consideration.

No one in Apple management thought Steve's project would ever amount to anything.

How much autonomy did he really have? Here's one example: the Macintosh factory. The Apple board was reluctant but finally agreed to give him a budget of $3 million for the plant. Before it was finished, Steve had spent $12 million. In just about any other company, so huge an overrun would have been grounds for any lesser figure than Steve to be fired, or the project would have been taken away. But those were the go-go days at Apple. The company was flush with capital from the sales of the Apple II, with nearly a billion dollars sitting in the bank. A $9 million overrun didn't seem like such a big deal.

Creating a Skunk Works

Of course, Steve wasn't the first person in business ever to conceive of a work group that would operate under different principles than the rest of the company. If Steve had needed a model, he could have found it in what came to be called the Skunk Works at Lockheed Aircraft. The head of that unit was Clarence "Kelly" Johnson, who had originally been hired as a tool designer. Kelly started off by advising the company's chief engineer that the design for the new Model 10 Electra aircraft was so flawed that the plane would be unstable in flight. Instead of firing him, the chief engineer allowed the youngster to do some wind tunnel tests. When the tests showed Kelly was right, he was pulled off tool design and given the job of redesigning the aircraft. He was reassigned as one of Lockheed's five aeronautical engineers.

In World War II, when the U.S. military grew alarmed that the new generation of German jet fighters would be far superior to anything we had, Kelly said he could develop a new fighter in six months. He was allowed to handpick the Lockheed engineers he wanted, setting them up in a make-shift but secret work area under a rented circus tent situated close to a smelly plastics factory. One of the design engineers answered his phone one day; because of the smell, he jokingly identified the location with the term from a popular comic strip: the Skonk Works. The label stuck, with *Skonk* becoming the more familiar *Skunk*.

The team, incredibly, created the new fighter, the P-38, under schedule and under budget. They were able to do this because Lockheed gave Kelly and his Skunk Works team latitude to ignore corporate operating procedures, break the rules, and do whatever it took to get the job done.

In the years that followed, the Lockheed Skunk Works teams, continuing to operate in secret and outside the standard corporate rules, would create one amazingly successful aircraft after another—planes as unique as the U-2 high-altitude spy craft.

Steve and Kelly were like-minded in their understanding of a simple truth: great products rarely get created in a bureaucratic environment.

Being Intrapreneurial

Steve began to call the Macintosh team *intrapreneurial*, a term that has since mostly faded from use but that was at the time coming into popularity in business circles.

Though the term is out of favor these days, at the time it seemed to Steve as made-to-order. The year after the Macintosh came out, he explained his understanding of that term to a *Newsweek* reporter as "[a] group of people going, in essence, back to the garage, but in a large company."[2]

If All of Apple Had Become a Skunk Works

Steve kept trying to influence the rest of Apple not to lose the entrepre-neurial spirit. He understood from the first that you don't create great products by passing a project along from one corporate division to another—a concept group, to a design group, to an engineering group, to a marketing group . . . or whatever. Without ever lecturing us about it, he believed in small, integrated teams. He had a vision of a team always small enough that every member—*every* member—stayed involved all the way through. Off-sites for the entire team would be one key way of making that happen. The commitments made at a meeting in front of all team members were sometimes even more powerful than a one-on-one promise to Steve; they were essential for keeping projects on schedule.

Yet even though he was the company cofounder and soon to become chairman of the board, trying to get the whole of Apple to shift to the model of a start-up was a struggle. I believe he already had the insight and inherent ability to turn all of Apple into a Skunk Works organization, yet the men running the company, and the board as well, didn't recognize this. So they stuck him off in the corner, thinking it was money well spent to keep him busy with Macintosh.

It's interesting to wonder about what would have happened if Steve had taken over Apple at the time. He would have killed the Lisa, which would have been a good thing. The Apple II/Apple III would have run out of steam. Apple would eventually have become a Macintosh company—much sooner than actually happened.

The Quest for Autonomy

I had come to Apple with some management skills I picked up in my years at IBM, where, for a time, I was part of that research team in San Jose developing what would become the forerunner of the ATM. The team included a unique group of engineers—very independent guys, trying to do their own thing. But *independent* wasn't a term in the IBM vocabulary. For every group like this, IBM always assigned a senior manager, supposedly a mentor but more of a monitor, to oversee the operation and keep it under control. Even though we were working in a research center, and actually called a Skunk Works unit, we were nowhere as free to operate as Steve Jobs was in his Macintosh days.

If you have your eyes set on creating autonomy within a larger company, you'll need to realize that the degree of freedom and independence Steve Jobs was able to wrest from Apple in some ways went a good deal beyond what is reasonable to expect in other situations. It helped that he had a champion supporting his cause: as a vice president, I was able to find ways of protecting the Mac group against attempts by the Apple bureaucracy to rein him in.

Off Course: An Argument with Peter Drucker

After the Macintosh had launched, I dropped by to visit a friend who was working on his PhD in business at the Claremont Graduate University in Southern California. At the time there was a lot of speculation about how Steve was going to get along at Apple. My friend picked my brain about this and the big question of whether Steve would be able to turn Apple around and keep the company from going under.

Over lunch, my friend introduced me to his adviser, the renowned Peter Drucker. At the time, Peter was in his late eighties and was one of America's most respected authorities in corporate management—an author, teacher, and consultant to many leading corporations. The question about Steve and Apple came up again. I said I was very confident in Steve's ability to get the whole company working like the teams of the Macintosh Pirate days, and that he would focus on the key products as his turn-around strategy.

This led to a conversation about what type of organization is most powerful for promoting innovation, as well as whether it was possible to foster a start-up mentality in an established company. The conversation between Peter and me grew heated.

His position was that among the numerous types of organization management structures, the *functional* organizational structure has been most successful—that is, a structure in which the organization is segmented into divisions like sales, marketing, human resources, engineering, manufacturing, and so on; this is what you might call a *top-down* or a *command-and-control* structure, based on subordination, with all orders coming from on high, passed down the ladder. Peter insisted that every company needs this type of structure to operate effectively and achieve its goals.

He rattled off a list of benefits. His list went something like this:

- The chain of command is structured and clear.
- The organized structure encourages guidance and teaching of subordinates.
- Having employees work in a silo with others who do similar work provides mutual support and learning.
- The structured organization provides a clear path for employees to move upward.

The major drawbacks as I saw them then and still see them include the following:

- The way a functional organization operates is based on structure, not process, which makes it very bureaucratic.
- The information flow, particularly between departments, is flawed and the processes are very complicated.
- Problems frequently take much too long to get resolved and are influenced by the politics of the organization.
- Teamwork is not emphasized and encouraged.
- Every major decision is the product of groups or committees; individual power is all but nonexistent.

Most important of all, the start-up type of structure encourages innovation.

Peter Drucker and I didn't settle anything that afternoon, but I still wonder if he would have revised his opinions had he lived long enough to see the full extent of Apple's success as an innovative, Pirate organization.

Checklist: Is Your Organization Pirates . . . or The Navy?

Do you have an organization that Steve Jobs would have approved of or, instead, one that would have pleased Peter Drucker? To determine how supportive your current organization is in fostering innovation, test yourself with this series of questions.

Is a climate of innovation continually supported by the board of directors, CEO, VP, and team leaders?

Any organization that wants to be fully innovative needs to have support for that innovation at every level, from the board of directors to the team leaders. This priority has to be continually communicated to all employees down to the newest hire and on display in every press release and public event.

Do you have the right people?

Not everyone who has spent his or her working life in traditional companies can really transform into the kind of independent thinker and performer that is so essential for an innovative team. Still, given the opportunity, most people are motivated to do what it takes to be creative. The right people will be very entrepreneurial in nature, have the ability to be flexible in their focus, and be able to change direction easily. The talent always needs to be open to change and open to the ideas of others. They need to be people who believe instinctively that the focus must be on the product, not the process.

Is there a method in place to monitor the team?

Steve was extraordinary in his hands-on managing of product development, at every level. I've never encountered the CEO of any other large company who was anywhere near as involved in the small details of each new product. It was as if Steve had invented the idea of ongoing development feedback on a regular, very frequent basis. In most cases, a new piece of design wasn't passed up the line to be shown to Steve by a VP; instead, the responsible team members themselves made the presentation. Steve didn't want any comments or instructions from him to be garbled as they were passed up the line, as in the old children's game of Telephone. The people doing the creative work got directly from Steve their praise or scolding, and directions on what he wanted changed or fixed.

Are your people strategic and focused at the same time?

This is where small, mobile teams are critical to the organization. Narrowing down certain broad goals into more specific tasks and organizing small teams to meet them is critical. Contributors need to have the big picture as well as how their function or job fits into the whole scheme: a designer working on the physical buttons of the iPod needs to understand the compelling reason the product is to have only one button. Steve's demands for secrecy, even among teams working on different parts of the same project, was sometimes in conflict with this goal, which in Steve's version turned into something like, "You'll get as much information as you absolutely need about what the other teams are doing, but not a syllable more."

Does your team have an absolute commitment to the product?

An absolute commitment to the product is the most important ingredient for innovative organizations. If your company makes products that everyone can use, are all your employees committed to using items from your company? Do they take pride in speaking about the product, not just to relatives and friends, but even to strangers?

Think of when Steve stepped onto the stage for a new product introduction. Every organization and contributor in Apple was probably impacted by his enthusiasm and commitment. It wasn't a sales head or product head on stage—it was the leader himself giving praise to the entire organization. When he said, "This is the greatest product in the world," everyone who had the remotest connection with developing, promoting, or marketing the product swelled with pride.

An Effective Structure Can Survive a Change of Command

One of the big advantages of the Apple-type organization is that it is based on products and on the innovators involved in developing and building those products, not on hierarchy or control. In a function-based organization, when there is change, particularly in upper management, it can have a profound impact through all levels. Since these organizations are built on control, the change can be dramatically negative.

But when Steve stepped down months before his death and his second-in-command Tim Cook became the new man in charge, the change had almost no impact on the organization. Prior to becoming CEO, Tim had been responsible for worldwide sales and operations plus the Mac division and played a key role in supplier relations. The change in command from Steve to Tim took place with barely a ripple on the waters.

The same was true with the departure of Ron Johnson, Apple's head of retail. Even though he was the real founder and implementer of the worldwide Apple store business—which his vision and Steve's design sense had made such a huge success against expectations—once again the transition was smooth.

This flexibility also applies to the board of directors. Shortly after Steve's departure, it was announced that longtime board member Arthur Levinson would become the chairman of the board. Meanwhile, Disney CEO Bob Iger was appointed as a new board member. Both have *Pirate* written all over them. Art was CEO of the multibillion-dollar biotech company Genentech and was sometimes referred to as the Steve Jobs of the pharmaceutical industry. He won numerous awards for his technical achievements as well as his leadership skills. Bob Iger, on the other hand, played an important role in rebuilding the partnership between Disney and Pixar after it appeared that the deal was down the tubes.

So despite these crucial changes, there is every reason to expect that Apple will continue to be the best model we have of what the successful Pirate company needs to look like: a comparatively flat organization, with a core made up of small teams of people focusing on *products*.

7

"No More Crap Products"

Creating Excellence

We used to dream about this stuff. Now we get to build it. It's pretty great.

—Steve Jobs

The reason for the outpouring of emotion around the world at the time of Steve's death was that his *products* had touched people emotionally. Money and profits were never the motivators for Steve. His motivation was, "I'm going to build a product for myself, a product that will fill a need and at the same time give me pleasure to use."

A product created from that vision sets the standard for the entire product category. Steve didn't invent the idea of building products that pleased the creator, any more than Leonardo da Vinci invented portrait painting with the Mona Lisa or carmaker Henry Ford invented the automobile. But Ford's cars drastically, dramatically, and beneficially changed American society, and that all happened because Ford was able to build reliable cars he could sell inexpensively. Steve, on the other hand, in all the years I knew him, never had *inexpensive* in his vocabulary.

No More Crap Products

When the LaserWriter was introduced—one of the first laser printers to make a splash and the one that set the standard—Apple still had on hand a large number of dot-matrix printers, which were by then outdated technology: they produced low-quality printouts and could not print graphics. Steve ordered them withdrawn from the sales channel and scrapped. He could hardly contain himself when he later found that they were still in the stores, still being sold. Steve's attitude was, "It's become a crap product. Get rid of them." The marketing people howled, "That would mean taking a big loss. We can move them out at a steep discount."

Steve understood that a lot of people would like the bargain of these inexpensive printers, even if the quality wasn't very good. He didn't care. He had the product focus, and that meant not selling inferior goods. "Blow them out," he ordered. He wanted every one of them dumped, regardless of how much money the company had to write off.

Steve went on to surround himself with people who understood and appreciated, or who already were living by, the product-focus concept. When he left Apple after the clash with management in 1985, that vision walked out the door with him. Apple became just another product company, where the only thing that mattered was numbers: sales, profits, stock price.

There was an aftermath to the dot-matrix affair: Steve said he wanted me to form a task force "to make sure we don't have any other crap products we should be getting rid of." I formed a task force to evaluate our process; the group included Joe Graziano, our chief financial officer; Debbie Coleman, the general manager of the Macintosh group; and Donna Dubinsky, director of distribution and sales administration.

I called this the Stop Crap Products Task Force; Steve *loved* that name. We launched into the task of evaluating every product that had an Apple logo on it, calling on the engineers who designed the product to come in and give us a presentation to justify what made it worthy enough to be in the Apple product line.

In addition, members of the task force would each take one of the products, try it out, and come back with their evaluation. If it was determined to be crap, instructions would go out to pull every unit off the shelf and get rid of it.

As part of this effort, Steve told me to get rid of the entire inventory of Apple III computers, which weren't selling and were only serving as a distraction from the Macintosh. The "entire inventory" consisted of 200,000 units of the Apple III, with price tags that ranged from $4,300 to $7,800. Do the arithmetic. This decision created quite a stir in Apple and in the press.

Seeing into the Future

A great music buff, Steve had been a huge fan of Sony's Walkman portable music player. But Sony didn't keep up with advances that new technology was making available. Steve's key people were doing a vastly better job of staying abreast. Software wizard Ruby Rubinstein learned of a tiny hard drive Toshiba had developed but hadn't found any customers for; hardly bigger than one-inch long, it could hold five gigabytes of data—a major technological breakthrough that would allow storing a thousand songs. In short order, Apple had an exclusive contract to buy the Toshiba drives.

With the smaller batteries that were becoming available, Apple would be able to make a very small unit that could keep playing for as long as 10 hours.

And the company already had its own data-transfer technology, Firewire, which would allow the player to download a ton of songs very quickly.

Put those elements together, and it's little wonder that Steve decided they added up to the ingredients of the first breakaway product under his leadership. Add a stunningly designed product package, and you have the iPod. It was a shining example of what Steve liked to call the company's "core strength." It was, as well, a shining example of how a complex device could be made easy for the user to understand and master. Nobody who saw it was surprised that the iPod was a worldwide hit from the day it was introduced. But more than that, it was the first evidence of the new Apple: entering a product arena brand new to the company by keeping abreast of the latest technology developments and embracing them ahead of competitors.

Yet with all those technology features, an important part of what made the iPod a must-have product was the aspect that grew out of Steve's and Jony Ive's shared passion for the physical appearance. It wasn't merely a technological wonder—the unit itself was breathtaking to look at, pleasing to hold, and pocket-size.

Steve wasn't just being cocky when he told reporters he wasn't concerned about efforts by Samsung and Dell and others to create competing devices. A *New York Times* article quoted Steve as saying that the Dells of the world don't spend money on design. "They don't think about these things," he said.[1]

The *Times* journalist, Rob Walker, drew from Steve a key acknowledgment that is worth printing out, framing, and hanging on your wall (I've reworded slightly to make it suitable for framing and hanging):

> **The starting point isn't a chip or a design;**
> **the starting point is the question,**
> **"What's the user experience?"**

What Customers and Competitors Can and Can't Tell You

Steve liked to say, "Customers can't tell you about the next breakthrough." That's part of the reason he didn't believe in market research: "Customers don't know the next big thing until they see it."

While the industry was busy trying to figure out the so-called tablet market, Steve kept his teams busy creating the iPad, so much ahead that it was virtually a brand new category and left everyone else playing catch up. That's what Steve did: He developed products, not concepts. There is not a lot of time or money spent by Apple on concepts. The Xerox PARC story highlights the downside of investing in concepts. Think of what Xerox could have been—the next IBM, Microsoft, or Apple! Good ideas drive good products, but only when they are part of an overall product vision.

Apple under Steve Jobs probably did less market research than any other major product company in the world. Steve loved the quote from Henry Ford, "If I had asked people what they wanted, they would have said 'faster horses.' "

Yet in the real world that the rest of us inhabit, you have to in some way get input in terms of how your product is being viewed in the market—how people are using it and what their issues are. Start by asking your customers.

Also, if you have competitors, what are they doing? Use the information, but don't get hung up on it. Near the end of his life, Steve violated this principle, which had been one of our operating principles from the very first, when he attacked Google over Android, the operating system for the Droid cell phones. Steve felt they had copied the principles of the iPhone software. He told biographer Walter Isaacson that Google was guilty of "grand theft," and that he was "willing to go to thermonuclear war on this." That was very un-Steve-like.[2]

If Steve and I had been writing down a set of operating rules, one of them would have been, "Figure out what you need to do to make your product better than your competitors' products." I think what happened was that Steve's products were so far ahead of the competition that he had never really needed to keep his eyes on what others were doing. So when Google came out with software that to Steve seemed like an imitation of the iPhone software, he found himself in a position that he had probably been in only once before, in a conflict with Microsoft. He didn't handle these situations well; he lost his cool and overreacted.

The principle of keeping an eye on your competitors in order to keep making your products better than theirs came out of a dinner that Steve and I had with Lee Iacocca, the head of carmaker Chrysler Corporation. Lee's view was, "We stay in touch with what General Motors is doing, we stay in touch with what Ford is doing, but we're going to do what we're going to do."

Don't Just Enter a Market, Build a Market

Leadership has to start with creating great products, things that contain a *wow* factor. At Apple it was not just about a new product; it was about creating a market or changing a market. Steve changed forever the entertainment market with the iPod, the way media is distributed with iTunes, the handheld media device that also makes calls with iPhone, and retailing with the way customers are treated in the Apple stores—to name just a few of his market changers.

Shortly before writing this chapter, I was in Korea again, this time at the invitation of Samsung, to talk about the Steve Jobs principles, and this was a central point of my discussion: You can't sustain your place in a market without market-changing innovation. That comes from the whole product, not just the hardware.

Becoming Your Own Best Customer

If you think about the iPod, the iPhone, the iPad, and even iTunes, these are all products in categories that already existed. The iPad, for example, was a tablet, and there wasn't anything new about bringing a tablet computer to the market. So what set it apart from all the others? As with all his other products, Steve kept it in development until all the technology was available to make it a great product, and his teams had come up with design solutions and user interface solutions that met his extraordinarily high standards. When the iPod was introduced, it set the new standard for all MP3 players.

That's what Steve did with each new addition to the lineup: He led his teams to create a product that he himself wanted to use. It's as if at each step he was asking himself, "What is still missing to make this a product that I want to own and use?" He would not say, "Okay, it's ready to be introduced," until it met his own personal standard. And that's why, each time, Steve's next new product set the standard for the category: he was his own ultimate consumer.

After Apple introduced the iPod, a Silicon Valley company known mostly for its storage products, SanDisk, came out with an MP3 player. Why? The SanDisk CEO, when asked some time later, gave an answer along the lines of, "Well, we got 3 percent market share."

Instead of asking, "How can we give buyers a great mobile music player?" or "What's our vision for creating a product that breaks new ground?" he justified the product in terms of capturing a minuscule share of the market.

Facing Up to Mistakes

I suppose all successful leaders learn from their mistakes. Steve was a master of that tactic, and his first major encounter with this was with the Macintosh. The advance publicity before the launch of the first Mac had been huge. Steve Jobs, this young, good-looking multimillionaire kid, had become a media favorite, making him the poster boy for the entire technology industry. Every time we turned around, he was on the cover of another major national magazine, with a full-of-praise interview. Unlike the secrecy Steve would later insist on for forthcoming products, the Macintosh was written about as opening a new era in computing. Praise was heaped on the product from every side.

January 24, 1984, when the Mac went on sale, was a keystone date in Steve's life and in the lives of every member of the Mac team. Yet Steve was quickly faced with a painful lesson. He had made some large and costly mistakes. By focusing so much on the user interface, he now realized, he had overlooked some crucial shortcomings. He had not put enough effort into getting software developers to write applications for the Macintosh. Customers who bought the machine could write letters on it, draft memos, write sales reports, and the like. And they could play some simple games that came with the machine. But there wasn't much else they could do with it. Some reporters wrote articles calling it a toy.

And then there was the disk-swap problem. Steve had insisted the Mac didn't need a hard drive. I remember one Apple executive, Betsy Pace, trying to write a last-minute speech on her Mac the night before she was to make a presentation to several hundred Apple people. She was working on one of those first-generation Macs. Without a hard drive and with limited internal memory, the computer had to store the text she was writing onto a floppy disk. Fine, except that every couple of paragraphs, the computer needed to get instructions from the software disk.

The disk she was using to store the text of her speech would pop out of the drive, and a message would appear on the screen telling her to insert the program disk—each time breaking her train of thought. After a few more paragraphs, the software disk would pop out, and the screen would call for the disk with the speech text to be reinserted.

And this happened every few minutes.

The price tag Steve had decided on early in the process would not cover the cost of a hard drive. That price was part of the dream of the machine he wanted to build, one that nearly everybody could afford. He had to face that he had been ignoring the realities. He and I talked a lot about this.

It was a lesson Steve learned well. From then on, in forming a vision for any new product, he was much more open to listening to input from all sources.

Many people who should know better can make these mistakes. I confess that even after my years of business experience, my years working with Steve, and products launched by companies I have started since my Apple days, I made one of these mistakes myself. In 2012, I introduced a new product to the marketplace, my Data Tunnel software tool for speeding up the transmission of very large files. In the design of the product, instead of keeping the user in mind, I listened to my technology experts. They designed a user interface that any technology guru could readily understand, except that the product wasn't being built for technology gurus; it was being built for everyday users.

I got a great deal of pushback from purchasers, and they were right: The user interface was terrible. We had to stop where we were and redesign the interface. Fortunately, we got it right the second time around, and the Data Tunnel product is now on the market and building sales momentum.

Another hurdle I have had to overcome: Sometimes you get painful criticism from a reporter you don't respect. There's always a great temptation to reject it out of hand and simply ignore it. But there have been times when I've been thankful for overcoming that instinct and allowing myself to recognize that some point the journalist had been making really was about a product flaw that I needed to address.

One of my early products, Migo, was the darling of the USB industry, drawing rave reviews from the likes of Walter Mossberg, a leading technology reporter for the *Wall Street Journal* and other periodicals. But then a review appeared in *PC Magazine* that was critical of the product, claiming that the software was difficult to launch and get ready to use.

I sat my teenage son down in front of the computer, pointed out the software, and said, "Try getting this started," knowing he would do it easily.

He failed. The complaint of the reviewer had been entirely valid. I had my software developer redo the start-up menu and the user guide.

Steve Describes His Product-Creation Process

In 2007, Steve introduced the iPhone to the world. In his very lengthy (but, as always, gripping) remarks, he described the motivation and process that led to the new phone. The following is Steve Jobs, verbatim, and it's worth studying because it provides one of the best views ever of how his mind worked. Note the language, as well—not at all the stuffy formality you would expect from the CEO of a giant global company. It's very *you and me*.

Steve Jobs:

Smart phones are definitely a little smarter, but they actually are harder to use. They're really complicated. Just for the basic stuff people have a hard time figuring out how to use them. Well, we don't want to do either one of these things. What we want to do is make a leapfrog product that is way smarter than any mobile device has ever been, and super-easy to use. This is what iPhone is. Okay?

So, we're going to reinvent the phone. Now, we're going to start with a revolutionary user interface. It is the result of years of research and development, and of course, it's an interplay of hardware and software.

Why do we need a revolutionary user interface? Here's four smart phones, right? Motorola Q, the BlackBerry, Palm Treo, Nokia E62—the usual suspects. And what's wrong with their user interfaces?

Well, the problem with them is . . . they all have these keyboards that are there whether or not you need them to be there. And they all have these control buttons that are fixed in plastic and are the same for every application.

Well, every application wants a slightly different user interface, a slightly optimized set of buttons, just for it. And what happens if you think of a great idea six months from now? You can't run around and add a button to these things. They're already shipped.

So what do you do? It doesn't work because the buttons and the controls can't change. They can't change for each application, and they can't change down the road if you think of another great idea you want to add to this product.

Well, how do you solve this? Hmm. It turns out, we *have* solved it! We solved it in computers twenty years ago. We solved it with a bit-mapped screen that could display anything we want. Put any user interface up.

And a pointing device. We solved it with the mouse. We solved this problem. So how are we going to take this to a mobile device?

What we're going to do is get rid of all these buttons and just make a giant screen. Now, how are we going to communicate this?

> We don't want to carry around a mouse, right? So what are we
> going to do?
>
> Oh, a stylus, right? We're going to use a stylus.
>
> *No!*
>
> Who wants a stylus? You have to get 'em and put 'em away, and
> you lose 'em. Yuck. Nobody wants a stylus. So let's not use a stylus.
>
> We're going to use the best pointing device in the world. We're
> going to use a pointing device that we're all born with—born with
> ten of them. We're going to use our fingers.

At this point in his remarks, I couldn't help remember how often in
meetings I had seen him studying his fingers, turning his hand this way and
that, clearly fascinated by the structure of the hand and by all the things a
human can do because we have been blessed with flexibility and those
opposable thumbs.

Steve continued:

> We're going to touch this with our fingers. And we have invented a
> new technology called multi-touch, which is phenomenal. It works
> like magic. You don't need a stylus. It's far more accurate than
> any touch display that's ever been shipped. It ignores unintended
> touches. It's super-smart. You can do multi-finger gestures on
> it. . . .
>
> We have been very lucky to have brought a few revolutionary
> user interfaces to the market in our time. First was the mouse. The
> second was the click wheel. And now, we're going to bring multi-
> touch to the market. And each of these revolutionary interfaces has
> made possible a revolutionary product—the Mac, the iPod, and
> now the iPhone. So, a revolutionary interface.

Those of us who were lucky enough to see Steve live on stage will never
forget how his passion for the product made him a fascinating, compelling
speaker—able to hold an audience absorbed, sometimes for an hour or even
two, and with such a casual, unrehearsed style that you would think he
was making it up as he went along, despite the many hours he had
spent fashioning the messages and preparing what he was going to say, do,
and show.

The Product Lineup: Saying No

Steve followed what I call his Say No principle with a passion. He came to understand that the challenge isn't which product ideas you decide to pursue, but which ones you decide *not* to. He was able to brag that Apple, which had become a $30 billion company, had fewer than 30 major products. But those 30 were what he had decided to pursue, after saying no to hundreds of others.

Think about that: over time, Apple had considered *hundreds* of product ideas before narrowing down to 30.

Learning from Failure

At the other end of the spectrum from the product history of Apple is the history of Kodak, the U.S. camera company founded in 1889 that was for many years the first name in photographic equipment and film stock. On the very day I began writing this chapter, Kodak filed for bankruptcy, and the reason the company failed is very striking.

One of Kodak's own people, Steve Sasson, in 1975 came up with a stunning new concept for taking still pictures: *digital* photography.[3] He was awarded a patent for it three years later. Yet Kodak, earning huge sums every year from selling of rolls of film, didn't pursue the idea. It was as if the company had said, "We have a lock on the market for film; why bother with this new-fangled idea that doesn't fit our vision?"

They are blaming the failure of the company on what they call cutthroat competition, but it was because they didn't have the vision to grasp that digital cameras could possibly capture virtually the entire market.

(A curious sidelight: The digital camera was made possible by a piece of electronics—the CCD, or charge-coupled device. One of the people on the team that invented the CCD, and who is credited with developing the process for manufacturing CCD-based chips, was Gil Amelio—the same man who, years later, as CEO of Apple, brought Steve Jobs back into the company. Small world.)

If you're not setting new standards for the market, don't be surprised if you arrive at a dead end like Kodak. Yes, a lot of companies are paying salaries to their employees and making money for their stockholders by doing look-alike products. But your vision needs to extend beyond that to something much grander.

8 More on Product Strategy

Design Is How It Works

Design is the fundamental soul of a man-made creation that ends up expressing itself in successive outer layers of the product or service. The iMac is not just the color or translucence or the shape of the shell. The essence of the iMac is to be the finest possible consumer computer in which each element plays together.

—Steve Jobs

Many people working under Steve in those early days didn't fully recognize what they were seeing. I recently ran into Dennis Matthews, who had been Apple's head of technical publishing years earlier. Referring to my first book, *The Steve Jobs Way*, he told me, "When I read your book, I got it. What hit me was that what we had been doing in those years [after Steve left] wasn't about the product. We were no longer a product company. We were doing functionality of technology. We were looking at things like how to build better software without asking, 'What will this mean to the user?'"

Product Development Decisions

Those comments of Dennis's reminded me of the project mentioned earlier that I had worked on during my years at IBM—designing the system that would sell tickets for BART, the Bay Area Rapid Transit, which was the high-speed rail transit system then under construction for the San Francisco area. The IBM project involved designing and building the machines that riders would buy their tickets from in each station. The concept required that you would have to register in advance and receive a personal code number. When you got to the station, you would enter your code and then feed coins or bills into the machine to purchase a ticket.

When the BART machines were pretty nearly finished, we told our employees to call on their family members and anybody else they could corral, to come in and try out the machines. On one Saturday, we must have had close to a thousand people show up to take part in our user trials.

It was a disaster, an unbelievable disaster. After feeding in your money, there was a long wait before anything happened. People would think the machine wasn't working and just start pushing buttons. Then they finally gave up and walked away, thinking they had lost their money.

The machines would only accept bills that were slid in with the correct orientation—face side up, the correct end of the bill going in first. If you slid the bill in wrong or if the bill was a little crumpled, the machine would slide it back out again. One more source of user frustration.

It took almost a year to redesign the system, work out the bugs, and get a user interface that made sense. Happily for us, BART wasn't ready on schedule, either; their delay gave us the time we needed to rethink our vision for the machines. The new, redesigned fare machines were ready in time for the opening of BART.

Those machines later became the prototype for the ATMs you now find at every bank, shopping mall, gas station, and just about everywhere in between.

But IBM doesn't make those machines, and there's a management principle to be learned from that truth. Steve Jobs was in the computer business. No one would have blamed him if he had held to that focus and kept Apple making nothing but computers. But he had a broader vision than that. He saw that the technological expertise of the company could be stretched in unexpected ways.

IBM, in contrast, did not want to have to deal with the consumer, and in fact refused to have the IBM logo appear on the BART ticket machines. (Though they did later get into the personal computer business, it went against the culture of the company, and they didn't stay in it.) Nobody at IBM recognized the vast opportunity offered by what became the global market for ATM machines. It was a product to be used by consumers and so didn't fit with how the company saw itself. I came to feel that this was a defining moment for IBM, a failure that led to the decline in IBM's fortunes.

When you're faced with a decision about a new product development that seems outside your current product arena, think like Steve Jobs—not like IBM. Stretch and apply your expertise in unexpected ways.

So how was Steve's approach different from the IBM mind-set?

Setting Standards: Design

Steve's concept of design was best captured in a line that he would sometimes throw at Apple teams that weren't meeting his standard: "Design isn't just what the product looks like or even what it feels like. Design is how it *works*."

Do you remember what it felt like to use an iPod for the first time? The iPod wasn't the world's first MP3 player—it was just the first to combine great looks with an interface that you knew how to use as soon as you picked it up. It just worked *intuitively*. As of this writing 10 years later, no company has an equivalent product, a viable competitor, for the iPod.

Remember that an eye-catching appearance is just one part of what needs to be a cohesive whole. Steve was the model of a man for whom there was no aspect of a product that was too small to do right.

Setting Standards: Simplicity

Another of Steve's leadership mantras was simplicity. As one prime example, he demanded that the iPod not have any buttons on it, not even an on/off switch. This seemed weird and undoable to the engineers working on the project, but Steve wouldn't bend. The engineers were pushed to their limits and finally stumbled on an idea that solved the problem: the scroll wheel. He used to talk about this as "one of my mantras," insisting that "simple can be harder than complex." Expanding on this idea to a journalist not long after he had returned from the NeXT detour, he said, "You have to work hard to get your thinking clean to make it simple. But it's worth it in the end because once you get there, you can move mountains."[1]

Setting Standards: Secrecy

When Steve returned to Apple, one of the values he demanded was absolute secrecy. It was drummed into new employees from the very first—incorporated in a very specific confidentiality agreement they had to sign, and stressed very strongly in the new-employee training. By then he had come to the vision of creating products with design and technology far ahead of what anybody else was doing. He understood very clearly that he couldn't jump the gun on other companies if Apple people in the know were even just a little careless about mentioning a detail here and a detail there. In an environment like that, your competition may turn out to be only a step behind in bringing out an imitation product that includes some of the best features of your latest hot new thing.

In addition, by that time he was convinced that you didn't ship great products by announcing a release date well in advance and then having to stick to it. You created great products by continuing to refine them until you were satisfied that every aspect—*every* aspect—had been honed to the point of meeting the very highest standards.

That's why Apple doesn't announce products months in advance.

There is a powerful side benefit of this strategy: the technology press and bloggers worldwide generate a great buzz with their guesses about what the next product or product upgrade will be—building greater and greater anticipation and millions of dollars' worth of free publicity until the launch date finally arrives.

For employees, this level of secrecy is uncomfortable. The Apple campus is like a fortress. The culture of secrecy runs so deep that Apple employees are careful about hanging out together after hours. And when outside their own workplace together with members of their team—even within the Apple campus—they avoid even whispering about what they're working on.

Even office space is changed to support a new project team. The carpenters appear and quickly put up new walls and security doors. These new protected spaces are called lockdown rooms. Information is so segregated that people working on one team of a new project are kept completely in the dark about what the other teams on the same project are doing, except for the pieces of specific information they may need for doing their own work effectively. The antenna team is told only what they absolutely need to know about the shape of the case. The team designing the case is kept in the dark about the software design. And so on.

The company understands, by the way, that it takes the secrecy thing a little far; there is a hint of humor about its loose-lips-sink-ships mentality. I was a little surprised when I first noticed a T-shirt on sale at the Apple employees' store with bold printing across the front that read:

> I VISITED THE APPLE CAMPUS
> BUT THAT'S ALL I'M ALLOWED TO SAY

Maintaining Control of Quality

Apple has been criticized for keeping a chokehold control over applications for the iPhone. I've never understood the criticism. Millions of people choose Apple products because they all know that anything that comes from the Steve Jobs factory is going to be miles better and phenomenally more satisfying to use than any competitive product. Steve understood without even needing to think about it that he could only maintain that quality with the iPhone if the apps available for it—being created by thousands of people outside Apple—met the high standards of the phone itself.

Compare that to the apps for Google's Android operating system that runs so many products made by iPhone competitors. Any teenager with a little time on his hands and a bit of technical or programming skill can create an Android app and make it available on the Android Market sites. A great many of the Android apps are poorly designed and not much good for anything more than frustrating the users. Google does not see this as a reflection on its own reputation and the reputation of the cell phone manufacturers that run the Google software. Their decision not to maintain control of the quality of the apps flies in the face of everything Steve Jobs stood for, and customers suffer the annoyance and frustration of trying to deal with applications that simply don't work.

Facing Up to Criticism

If you manage to conceive of a radically new product and bring it to market while remaining true to your vision, be prepared for the likely onslaught of criticism. Steve experienced that when the Macintosh was first introduced. The same thing happened again years later. So-called experts and journalists warned that Apple was making a huge and costly misstep when Steve announced the first Apple store. The company had zero experience in retailing, which is a notoriously difficult field to survive in, let alone show a significant profit; established, nationwide retail chains go out of business regularly because they are unable to remain profitable.

But once Steve had the vision of what he wanted to do and had made certain that his instincts aligned with his goal, he stuck by his decision and followed his gut.

And what happened? As Apple opened more and more stores, the critics changed their tune. I noted earlier that on a per-square-foot measure, the Apple stores were generating far more sales than any other national retail chain in the United States. That was true even though discount retailers were selling the same Apple products at reduced prices!

The moral is, make your goal something you strongly believe in, make certain you have a clear vision of how it will benefit your customers, process enough information to confirm you are moving in the right direction, and then stand by your decisions.

And be prepared to withstand the criticism of people who don't have the facts and the determination that you do.

Steve's Legacy: The Power of the User Interface

Every January in Las Vegas, tens of thousands of technology people gather in a vast convention hall for the Consumer Electronics Show (CES), which has been the largest industrial show held anywhere in the world. In 2012, I was struck by what I saw there. It was as if Steve Jobs had been consulted by one company after another after another to help them conceive and craft products that were born out of a clear corporate vision. Sure, I was seeing plenty of the usual run-of-the-mill, copycat "Our competitor has one of these, so now we're offering our own just to keep up." But I was also seeing plenty of Apple-inspired products that showed a true vision.

And what was the distinguishing mark of the *vision* products? Easy: a well-thought-out, well-conceived user interface. At one booth after another, people were actually using that term: user interface.

In other words, ease of use—which also includes users being readily able to understand what they can do with the product. Think what the telephone became in our lives. It became a device run by incredibly complex technology, yet you never have to think about the technology. When the phone rings, you just pick it up and answer—you don't even give it a second thought.

In a similar way, when you get in your car, you turn the key and just drive off. You don't need to know anything about the flow of gasoline into the engine, or the pistons driving up and down, or adjusting the gas/air mixture, or how the drive force gets from the engine to the wheels. The fascination Steve Jobs had for cars was part of this emphasis, and he wanted to make the Macintosh and every Apple product since then just as simple and obvious as starting a car and driving away.

As a result, every product Apple created under Steve is so intuitive, it becomes so much a part of you, that you hardly need to think about it in order to be able to use it effectively. The inner workings become invisible. That's why his products are usable among a range of people, from kids as young as five to people in care facilities for the elderly.

That was one of the crucial things Apple lost in the years that Steve wasn't there. The company began working in what I saw as the Microsoft model. They became caught up in building pieces of technology to make the products work, instead of always asking, "How is this going to help the user?" and "How can we design this feature so users will discover it and figure out for themselves how to use it?"

Looking Ahead

Those products you have in development right now or the one product you're betting on so heavily—how close can you come to creating a new standard?

Sure, it's a tough target to aim for. You and I both know that in their entire career, most people will never achieve this goal in a single thing they do. The much-admired Apple consultant and coach Arynne Simon used to say, "If you don't aim for the sky, you'll never hit the bell tower."

9 Entrepreneurial Confidence and High Standards

My job is to not be easy on people. My job is to take the great people we have and to push them and make them even better, coming up with more aggressive visions of how it could be. . . . My job is to make the whole executive team good enough to be successors, so that's what I try to do.

—Steve Jobs[1]

Some people are lucky enough to find a mentor who plays a big role in shaping their personal management style and validating their beliefs. Steve found a mentor in Bob Noyce, who was one of the pioneers of today's technology as co-inventor of the microchip and cofounder of a leading manufacturer of the chips, Intel. I worked with Bob at Intel and in hindsight believe he may have been the closest visionary to Steve, and Steve's best example of what it means to be the leader of a development team.

Bob's perspective was, "You can't really understand what's going on now unless you understand what came before." I always felt that Steve's leadership style was the kind of thing that you can't learn in a classroom but that he came to intuitively. I would define it as an absolute commitment to the product, supported by an intuition for leading people.

Swagger

Steve had a certain swagger about him and was often accused of being very brash about his views of the future. But in fact he was a very shy person and this brashness was his way of expressing his commitment to his vision for the future.

In accompanying Steve to CEO meetings in Silicon Valley and to Stanford, I discovered that his swagger, his sense of self-assurance, when talking about the future of technology was almost overwhelming. Students loved it, but a lot of CEOs were not that happy.

Steve and I were once at a CEO luncheon in Palo Alto that the leaders of Intel were also attending. At one point, Steve commented, "The big problem with Silicon Valley and developing new products is old thinkers." As for his own outlook, "I never trust anyone over 40 years old." (Though around Apple he used to say, "Never trust anyone over 40, except Jay"—which of course pleased me as a huge compliment, but it also was a challenge, a reminder of what I needed to live up to.) Andy Grove took great exception to Steve's remark, particularly since everyone in the room, except Steve, was over 40! Steve may have been one of the wealthiest people in the room but that did not alter his opinion of the future. And he always brought an entrepreneur's energy with him.

Sometimes it's not what you say but how you say it. Steve's swagger was never more apparent than at product launches, where he would hold the audience spellbound. But his swagger was about the product, not himself, and that's where his product leadership was most apparent.

An Enthusiastic Leader

Steve Jobs is almost universally thought of as one of the most inspiring and charismatic business figures in history. Every person in a leadership role wants to be charismatic, and the first step in becoming a charismatic leader is to be enthusiastic about what you do. Real—not forced—enthusiasm is tangible and transfers naturally to others, who cannot help but become more enthusiastic themselves. This leads to a more synergistic team.

Steve's enthusiasm came from his strong entrepreneurial will, combined with risk-taking and the ability to act quickly, with absolute conviction that you are doing the right thing. When you're able to do this, people will be willing to follow your lead.

The Power of *No*

Steve had an uncanny ability to make decisions that were both instantaneous and solid—often to the utter frustration of his engineers. Sometimes his decisions seemed arbitrary, like not having more than a hundred people on the Mac team—based on his claim that he couldn't remember everyone's name if there were any more people than that.

He also had product boundaries. When we visited Sony and they showed us hundreds of products, Steve warned Sony cofounder Akio Morita that they had way too many, so many that customers had to be getting confused.

It was the threat of customer confusion that drove Steve to say no—No Newton, no licensing of Macintosh technology for other companies to make Mac clones, and so on. These were obvious examples of making sure our product boundaries fit our ultimate vision for the product family. Steve had the reputation of being a micromanager; he was, but it wasn't arbitrary. It was for a very good reason: he was looking out for the customer.

I read a story once in *Fast Company* magazine about a group that came to Apple prepared with page after page in a presentation about a new feature for the Mac, for burning DVDs—copying music or videos from the computer to a DVD disk. Steve saw a few slides, with mocked-up screen shots and various menus along with engineering documentation.

About two minutes into the presentation, Steve said, "No, you don't get it." He went to the whiteboard, drew a small rectangle, and said something like, "Here's how it needs to look. It's got one window, you drag the icon of your video into the window, and you click the button that says Burn. That's it." He got up and left.

A *no* from Steve was usually final. For the most part, the only exception was when one of his team members or team leaders could come back with a compelling, convincing reason for him to change his mind. Sometimes that took guts, especially if you were at a lower working level—and you damned well had better be able to explain your reasoning briefly but in a compelling way. But Steve *did* listen, and did sometimes change his mind.

The Virtues of Small Teams

Steve deeply believed that to drive excellence in an organization, you need not just talent but small teams, like that cap of a hundred people for the Mac team: When there was an essential need for another person, a current team member had to be moved to some other part of Apple.

As for his story of setting that limit because he couldn't remember the names of more than a hundred people on a team—nobody was fooled. Though the actual number was arbitrary, his real motivation was that he could not keep closely in touch with the work being done if there were too many people for him to supervise personally.

When the iPhone was being developed, the iPhone team was quartered in a separate building, both to keep the team cohesive and to protect their work. But at the same time, a leader needs to recognize that the small teams have to be able to interact on lots of issues with people from the rest of the organization.

A Leadership Challenge

Innovation has nothing to do with how many R and D dollars you have in your budget. When Steve's team developed the Mac, IBM was spending at least 100 times more on R and D. It's not about money. It's about the people you have, and how you lead.

Steve never faced a greater leadership challenge than when he returned to Apple. He had to turn himself into a leader who could establish methods to manage a complex strategic change in direction. Holding on to the Mac computer when he returned to Apple was one of these decisions. His predecessors had tried to sell the software, sell through distributors, and encourage other companies to license the technology and manufacture clones of the Mac. The idea of allowing other companies to offer inferior, lower-quality versions of the Mac or to market ill-designed products based on the Mac operating system simply wasn't in Steve's concept of how the universe should work. It simply didn't match his mantra of always giving customers the best products you could conceive and create. Imitations by companies that didn't adhere to Steve's high standards would contradict everything he stood for.

Steve's strategy was not about market share or finances; it was finding the next great product for his customers.

Evangelizing Innovation

I keep coming back to the subject of innovation because it underlies so much of learning to be Steve-like.

Creating an environment that supports and encourages innovation is one of your most important roles as a leader. A Pirate team or Pirate company like the original Macintosh group is a fertile setting for this, but leaders need to remember the symbolic power of their actions. Again, Steve was as proud of the many products and product ideas that he gave the axe to over the years as the ones that he pursued and made into great successes—knowing that it can be tougher to say no and kill a promising idea than to say yes, and find yourself trying to do so many things at once that none of them are done to the highest standard of quality that Steve always insisted on.

One of my favorite stories of Steve encouraging innovation—or, rather, I should say *demanding* innovation—vividly illustrates his level of involvement in details of a product that most anyone else would have taken for granted. When he was shown an early model of the iPod, he said it was too large. His developers explained that they had used the absolute minimum size of case that would hold all the necessary components.

Steve carried the device to a fish tank and dropped the iPod into the tank. As it sank, a stream of air bubbles gurgled to the surface. Steve gestured to the bubbles and pointed out that if things were really packed tightly inside, there would not be any space left for the air that was streaming up. The team went back and made the iPod smaller.

Some other examples:

The night before the opening of the first Apple store, Steve didn't like the look of the floor tiling. He had the tiles ripped up and the job redone.

Right before the iPod launched, he had all the headphone jacks replaced so that they were more clicky—the *click* sound assuring the user that the connection had been made.

These kinds of involvement in details by the leader send unmistakable signals about the expectation of innovation.

Inspiration comes from example, not just from words. One of America's greatest football coaches, the revered Vince Lombardi, once said, "Leadership is based on a spiritual quality—the power to inspire, the power to inspire others to follow."

Employee Owners

Rewarding the Product Stakeholders

You can't talk about profit; you have to talk about emotional experiences.

—Steve Jobs

On our long walks together around the Apple buildings, Steve hardly ever talked about himself (except, on rare occasions, about his relationship problems), and he talked about other people almost exclusively in terms of their work and ideas, or about how to deal with some particular person who was in some way not measuring up. Mostly, the conversation was focused on products and on Apple.

During one of these walks in the early days, Steve and I explored the possibility of turning Apple into an employee-owned company. I thought, "Wow, will the board go crazy over *that* idea!" But I had to agree that this would make Steve's emphasis on the product even more successful. However, based on the feedback we got, it seemed almost impossible to make this happen, particularly with large blocks of Apple stock held by a few people. But it certainly made sense for the type of company we wanted to build.

Steve always admired United Parcel Service (UPS), the global delivery company with the familiar brown trucks. (In Venice, deliveries are made by UPS boats painted in the same brown color.) The attraction for Steve was that UPS is one of the most notable employee-owned companies. Originally started by two teenagers as a message delivery service in 1907—before most people had telephones—it has since 1945 been mostly owned by its employees.

Early ownership was mostly management and supervisory personnel, but UPS eventually included the entire workforce that now numbers over 300,000. The company expanded its shares to all full-time employees through share purchase programs and the ability to convert retirement funds to stock. The purpose of these programs was to have its employees take direct responsibility for the customers' satisfaction. UPS found that the program allowed them to give employees greater decision-making latitude, which in turn allowed for reducing the number of supervisors. It also allowed building more time into the day for customer needs. Again, a product-driven approach to ownership.

I happened to be in Rye, New York, once on a business trip in 1999 when UPS went public. The pub I was at was a local center for employee celebrations of the public offering. I thought, *Damn, if we had done this at Apple, the employee owners would have voted to make Steve the head of the company, and he would never have left.*

Stakeholders

When people talk about the stakeholders in a company, they are referring to the stockholders and, sometimes, the holders of options. At UPS, Apple, and many other companies, stakeholders also include those employees who own shares of stock or options in the company. That's standard, of course, for the top level; having a large part of the workers as stakeholders is much less common.

Unlike almost any other executive, Steve Jobs was never focused on profits, share price, or whether the stock market price of company shares was going up or down. His focus was instead on which product ideas to pursue and then making those few products as near perfect as humanly possible in every way.

In a product-driven company like Apple, the product stakeholders are incredibly important to its success. But the attitude at Apple is significantly different: Focus on making the products successful, and financial success will follow.

Making sure that Apple employees benefited financially from their role in helping to create great products was a very important issue to Steve. We spent a lot of time figuring out how to implement programs that made the product success everyone's success. In Steve's words, "With great products will come great rewards to all of us."

All employees who went to work at Apple got stock options on their first day of employment. Also all employees were eligible for profit sharing and bonuses—so all Apple employees were stakeholders. From the receptionist to the senior engineers to the senior vice presidents, we all had a stake in the company. By this model, companies provide value for those involved in adding value to the company.

What's important about a product stakeholder reward system is that it is truly tied to the accomplishments of individuals and the product. This is not about years of service to the company or your birthday; it's about meaningful accomplishments that push the overall strategy of the company ahead.

As an example of taking product performance into account, Steve got a bonus program implemented in 2002, despite the company missing its stated revenue and profit targets for the bonus program. Apple awarded employees in its incentive program a special recognition bonus amounting to between 3 and 5 percent of their base salary. Top management including Steve were excluded from the program.

All the rewards and bonuses were based on product achievements, not on financials.

Ownership

Another way Apple rewarded employee stakeholders was through stock options and stock discount programs.

The stock option grant, popular and widely used in the United States and elsewhere, allows an employee to buy a certain number of shares in the company at an attractive price. When employees are shareholders, they benefit when the stock goes up, which obviously gives them a financial incentive for seeing the company be successful.

One of the unique stock option programs in industry is offered by coffee retailer Starbucks, which I've mentioned earlier for its dedication to its customers. Starbucks emphasizes the relationship between store employees and customers by calling its employees *partners*. The stock option program for Starbucks also includes part-time employees, a unique feature. The company believes its success is directly tied to the respect it shows partners on a daily basis. I have to admit that after going to a Starbucks in my neighborhood a few times, I was surprised to get the welcome, "Hello, Jay, what do you want today?" Very Apple store-like.

The Starbucks Direct Purchase Plan allows employees to buy shares at a discount, with deductions out of their pay or tax-qualified plans.

In contrast, when I started my employment at IBM in 1970, IBM stock was at $440 a share and with my small starting salary, I could only buy two shares a year. Not much incentive there.

It's the "Thanks"

Employee recognition is a widespread practice but at Apple, it was focused on recognizing people's contribution to the product. Organizing how to say thank-you and when can make a big difference. The $100 bill Steve handed out to all the manufacturing employees at the factory along with his simple "Thank you" when the first Mac rolled off the assembly line is an example of what I'm talking about.

When you recognize people the right way, it reinforces what type of performance you are intent on making standard in the organization. There is something about a crisp $100 bill handed out by the CEO that is magic. We also believed that it had to be recognition for the entire team, not just for selected individuals. That made a huge difference.

Another unique Apple thank-you story: When the company went public, Woz walked the halls handing out some of his stock certificates to employees as his way of showing appreciation.

The employees at the Apple stores during the launch of the iPhone 4 were kept in good spirits by company-provided food—according to my source, "good food." The New York store on Fifth Avenue, one employee said, provided a masseur for overworked employees during one of the launches—like a Steve Jobs Zen thing.

Saying thanks is not just a nice thing to do but a communication tool that reinforces the most important outcome you want for your business; it multiplies your investment in the business.

T-Shirts, T-Shirts, T-Shirts

One thing that has always amazed me was the power of the T-shirt at Apple. I had a closet full of about 40 of them from various functions and events. There was even a book published with pictures of many more than that number, including one that executive coach/speechwriter Arynne Simon used to hand out that said, "Don't Should on Me." (She taught that telling someone what they *should* do is manipulative and makes the other person uncomfortable.)

But the importance of T-shirts is how they are distributed and for what type of recognition. The idea of using a themed T-shirt at Apple to celebrate an event or promote a theme began with one that trumpeted the launch date of Mac. These shirts were designed with the graphics look of the Macintosh and proudly displayed on the sleeve what was then the intended launch date: May 15, 1983. They became famous and much coveted.

On the day the announcement was to be made of the launch date, the entire team gathered in the atrium to celebrate by downing bottles of Odwalla juice and receiving their new Mac T-shirt.

Later that month, Steve wanted to offer Mac T-shirts to the board members. I went to the meeting with him, toting a box of the shirts. At the end of the meeting, he announced, "Please help yourself to a T-shirt." I thought, *These titans of industry aren't going to care about getting a T-shirt.*

Was I ever wrong!

There was almost a stampede to get a shirt. It was like a once-a-year sale at a discount store. They not only wanted one for themselves but for their wives and kids, too. The shirts were gone in a minute, with the board members all but fighting over them. I told Steve after the meeting, "Maybe we're in the wrong business. Let's hope there'll be as big a demand for the Mac!"

Even today, the dress of the staff in an Apple store is an Apple T-shirt. I was recently in a store and witnessed an event that I thought was great: An employee was starting her first day. She was escorted through the store while all the other employees applauded her; at the end of that parade, her new T-shirt was tossed to her, while everybody called out, "Welcome aboard!"

I was at a meeting recently at Google and noticed that near the reception area were boxes of T-shirts for employees. It was a help-yourself system of distributing recently printed shirts. What struck me about this is that at Apple, the T-shirts were always used to celebrate a product event, meeting a schedule, introducing new technology, achieving an impressive number of Mac users, or some other notable event. It wasn't just about getting a free shirt. That was what made the Apple T-shirts so memorable: they were part of the thank-you culture.

Let's Party

A critical process of keeping the employee spirit alive was the timely parties at Apple. Of course, the theme and size of the party was dictated by what was being celebrated. In addition to the expected T-shirts, there would often be some other memorable gift that made the moment unique. In the early days, musical entertainment was always at the center of the events, with Steve's favorite group, a soul/rhythm-and-blues band called Jack Mack and the Heart Attack, often the band of choice. The party might be an afternoon celebration for meeting a product milestone, or just donuts and coffee when you arrived in the morning; it was the thought that counted. All these events were team oriented, reflecting that most important part of the Apple culture: the team comes first.

The *let's party* idea was something we had picked up from another Silicon Valley company, Tandem Computer. Under the guidance of founder James Treybig, Tandem had around-the-pool beer parties on Friday afternoons to celebrate the week's accomplishments. Before then, the Valley had been dominated by IBM and HP, which were very much not partying companies.

In 1983, Apple hit a sales level that would generate a billion dollars a year, so we had a major party on Bandley Drive to celebrate the incredible growth that Apple had achieved and to recognize the employees who helped make it happen. We had a special set of glass goblets designed for the occasion and had a big block party with food, drink, and of course Steve's band of choice.

One of the most memorable parties we had was for the 1985 Super Bowl, played nearby at the Stanford Stadium—the year after the Super Bowl with the "1984" ad. By arranging for Apple to donate money for the restoration of the stadium, we were given over 1,000 tickets for the game. I used these to recognize the various groups in Apple—from development, to sales, to PR—for their work in the Mac launch. With Super Bowl tickets being among the most coveted and sought after, the gift was an Apple thank-you that no one ever forgot.

Continuing the Tradition

Now that the company has its own retail outlets, it includes customers in company celebrations. May 2011 marked the 10th anniversary of the Apple stores, and the company decided to celebrate the 10 years by introducing to customers to a whole new retail experience called Apple Store 2.0—a name suggesting that the stores are, to Apple, in the same class as every one of the carefully nurtured products: due for regular upgrades. The 2.0 stores included start-up sessions for new customers, along with the introduction of new sound systems.

Just as everyone on the Mac team was given a Mac with their name on the front of it as recognition of their contribution to making the product happen, Steve did the same thing, only better, when the iPhone was introduced: this time around, *every* employee—including the many people working in the Apple stores—was given a new iPhone.

At the center of this tradition were the huge discounts for employees at the Apple employees' store on the campus in Cupertino. Besides buying for themselves, employees can buy computers and other Apple products at significant discounts in limited quantities for a friend or family member. There was also a way to recommend a donation to a school, so many computers were directed to the schools of employees' children. Think what it means to an Apple parent to go into a school and see an Apple computer on the kids' desks, as well as in the school's computer lab. This is another form of recognition that hasn't brought much public attention but is very highly appreciated by Apple people.

Steve was tough at times, but he certainly knew how to show his appreciation in ways that inspire.

The Apple Workplace

Fostering Creativity

I'm actually as proud of many of the things we haven't done as the things we have done.

—Steve Jobs[1]

Steve was always looking for ways to nurture creativity. He had been inspired by the HP Way culture at Hewlett-Packard, and it had become a guiding light for him. His connection to HP went back a long way. As a teenager, Steve had written a letter to the cofounder of Hewlett-Packard, Bill Hewlett, requesting parts to build some sort of counter. Hewlett provided Steve with the parts, gave him advice on building the device, and offered him a summer job.

One day I suggested to Steve that we adopt a program that I was very familiar with from IBM: bringing in outside speakers—professors and business leaders—to help us develop a course that would highlight the way we wanted the leadership at Apple to lead, sort of the Apple Way. As a sidelight of developing this idea came the concept for Apple University, which would be a "university without walls." We would invite some of the greatest thinkers and leaders to help in supporting the concept of the Apple

Way. Though Apple already had a new employee orientation program, we had no leadership training.

Apple University

Steve and I imagined a university that would promote novel management ideas, have a staff of people who were unique for the new type of corporation, and would be able to offer advice and counsel to its participants. Some of what we lined up was unique in corporate history. First, we had some very prominent professors, including Rosebeth Moss Kanter, who held (and still holds) the Arbuckle Professorship at Harvard Business School, where she specializes in strategy, innovation, and leadership for change. Her book *Change Masters* had caught my eye and made me believe she could help and could fit into the Apple culture. Her book was about how innovation had to become the key in American industry. In those days it was projected that the typical American family would soon have a Toyota in the garage and several Sony products in their home. I knew her take on this would really resonate with Steve.

We also had to find a new style of training that would fit our needs to be open. I saw a segment of the popular television investigative program *60 Minutes* where a woman, approached on the street, was taught how to play tennis in 15 minutes by the author of *The Inner Game of Tennis*, Tim Gallwey. This book was about not getting caught up in how you thought you were supposed to hit the ball. Tim had found ways to focus the mind of the player on direct and nonjudgmental observation of the ball, the body, and the racquet in a way that would speed learning, heighten performance, and enhance the enjoyment of the process.

When Tim came to Apple, he taught me to play a game called bounce hit, and I was playing great tennis in about one hour.

Another one of our many Apple U professors was Jim Whittaker, the first American to climb Mount Everest. Even though he and his Sherpa, Nawang Gombu, ran out of oxygen, they managed to reach the summit. Once there, Jim became the first American to plant the U.S. flag. In 1965 he guided Robert Kennedy up the newly named Mount Kennedy in Washington. He was a freethinker, a risk-taker, and someone who could inspire even Steve Jobs.

We always completed the Apple U programs with an Outward Bound adventure that involved making your way through a course of ropes, trees, and hazards, teaching participants not only survival skills but also inter-personal teamwork and leadership skills.

Another part of Apple U was our leadership speaking program where we would bring in CEOs from other corporations to speak to the upper management of Apple. Part of my motivation in developing this program was to have Steve meet other industry leaders/CEOs one-on-one, to get some ideas about leadership from them. The two of us would meet with the CEOs for dinner the night before their presentation to the management team.

At almost all these dinners, Steve dominated the conversation, so not much leadership knowledge came out of it for him, though he did hear many valuable ideas. We had corporate leaders such as Fred Smith from Federal Express, Lee Iacocca from Chrysler, Bob Crandell from American Airlines, and Jim Henson, creator of the immensely popular Muppets television show. It was a very good program for the executives of Apple, even if it didn't do much for Steve's leadership style.

Another part of Apple U was the individual coaching we did for the executives. The most valuable and beloved of these coaches was the late Dr. Arynne Simon. Arynne had a unique style that I have never seen matched before or since. She believed that inside each of us was a basic goodness and decency, and that was where her coaching started. She aimed through her coaching and developing leadership skills to integrate humanity and productivity.

I was the gatekeeper for Apple U, and I was skeptical about this type of coaching, but Arynne's impact on me and many Apple executives was permanent.

In a conversation with Steve not long before he first became ill, he said, "Jay, one of the many things I remember about your accomplishments at Apple was Apple U."

"It was fantastic," he said.

I felt the kind of warmth we all do when we're rewarded with special praise, but it made me realize how rare praise was from Steve. My memory skipped back to the one other time he had lavished me with a precious compliment. In the 1984 Apple annual report, a one-of-a-kind masterpiece that set the standard for excellence in corporate annual reports, he highlighted what he considered the top creative corporate organizations in Apple. One of those was the group I headed, human resources, which he acknowledged for the Apple University program. It was the only time I was ever aware of that Steve bestowed compliments for creativity on adminis-trative groups.

The First Day

Another of Steve's leadership ideas for nurturing creativity grew out of his recognition that new hires need to become quickly integrated into the Pirate way of thinking. Over a couple of months, he and I kicked around a number of ideas for doing this. Following the guidelines we worked out, I set up several tools, beginning with the newbie's arrival on campus.

The new employees' orientation program was designed to start implanting the Apple culture from the very first. Apple employees went through the new employee orientation program their first day on the job, with discussions about some of the programs, Apple history, and an inside look at how Apple operates.

The newcomers received the usual sort of information packet, an Apple T-shirt (to some readers that might sound a little tacky, but, as I've said, they were *very* popular), and an Apple sticker.

(I always laughed about those stickers. As a prank, when we took an airline flight, on deplaning we'd leave one on the back of an airplane seat. And as a taunt to IBM, once when I was in Paris on business, my walk from the hotel in the morning would take me past the IBM office building; I'd paste one of the Apple stickers on their door, then check on the following morning to see if it was still there. One time, the sticker remained on the door for four days—leaving me to wonder if the French IBMers were really that unobservant or just didn't care.)

The second part of the orientation was to understand the products and master them. In the early days of Apple, the new employees were given an Apple II to take home for their own use. The only catch was that a month later there would be a test on using the product. If you failed, you would be terminated. The pass rate was 99.9 percent.

In Apple today new employees are given a computer and expected to be able to connect it to the network—even though no IT manager likes the idea of non-IT people hooking up to the company's network. But if you are hiring the best, then they should be able to pass any test you give them about your products.

The Buddy System

It was also important for new employees to be connected to people who really understood the Apple culture, so we would assign each new hire to someone in the organization—someone the person did not know—who would become the newbie's "buddy." The buddy's job was to give answers and provide support or reassurance as needed, whenever the new hire had questions or concerns about Apple or his own job. The buddy was also available for more mundane things like helping the newbie learn her way around the building and the campus.

The buddy can be very valuable in helping the newcomer get through this awkward period. We would try to have buddies who were in another organization; a new programmer, for instance, might be assigned a buddy from the marketing organization. (After Steve's return, he changed the name to iBuddy, for a reason that every Apple follower will understand.) I marvel that a program Steve and I started over 30 years ago is still relevant today. Although in today's Apple secrecy is so paramount that some new hires are assigned to a cubicle in a different work area until their manager has enough confidence in their sense of security that they can be allowed to begin knowing about the work of the team they're joining.

Creating an Innovative Organization within a Navy Company

In the middle of 1970, the management of IBM asked me to take charge of designing a facility where all of IBM's development programming talent and resources would be pulled together. It would have to be a place that could accommodate about 2,000 people. I was to assemble a task force to work with me in dreaming up and bringing to life a facility that would stimulate innovation, creativity, and social interaction.

I put together a group of IBM programming managers and programmers from coast to coast, and we worked together to conceive the best environment for programmers to work in, based on their own experience plus input from the employees in their own workgroups. Each of the 10 people in my group would have a single vote: there would be no pulling rank by the more senior people. Once my team had arrived at the design parameters, those would become the list of requirements that would be turned over to the architects.

Some of the key points the team arrived at form the basis for a list you might consider in planning a space for a team of innovators:

Team Common Areas

The programmers strongly expressed the need for spaces where team members could work together in discussions and brainstorming. These common areas would have amenities to stimulate thought and even a setup to allow for presentations by one or two members to the whole team.

Privacy

In addition to the common area, each member would have his own individual workspace, where he could concentrate free of distractions.

View

Though it may at first seem a contradiction to the privacy requirement, the consensus was that each programmer's office or private area should have a window, giving a view of the outside world. And that view was not to be an adjacent building or a parking lot, but some serene part of nature. So the immediate surroundings of the building would have to be handsomely landscaped, and the pressure would be on to find a setting that looked out on mountains or distant hills. The natural environment, I learned, was very important to programmers. (In the setting finally chosen, some of the windows looked out on a nesting area for bald eagles. It doesn't get much better than that.)

Interacting with Other Teams

Programmers also wanted opportunities to rub shoulders with programmers of other teams. We called for the cafeteria to be designed in a way that encouraged people to sit at random, free to join people they didn't work with.

After months of research, opinion gathering, and deliberating, our final set of criteria for the lab called for a circular building with seven interconnected towers. Some 75 percent of the offices would have windows that looked out on nature, with all of the offices designed to be approximately the same size. At the ground level, the towers would surround an open space similar to the quad of Harvard and a few other major universities. Since the lab would be located in a rural area, we called for convenience services including a dry cleaners and a company store that would offer all kinds of personal items.

In late 1970, I presented the findings of my task force to the chairman and board of directors of IBM. The facility was approved, to be built in Northern California. Originally known as the Santa Teresa Labs, it was IBM's first-ever development center built for software development and the first major IBM facility to be located outside of the headquarters area in upstate New York.

Opened in 1978, it was the most beautiful place I've ever worked. Following the guidelines my team had developed, 90 percent of the campus, including the hills in the background, was set aside as open space. But this tribute to nature wasn't just left open for the IBM researchers to appreciate the natural beauty. A large part of the flat area was turned into a working orchard leased out to a farmer, and the hilly area was leased to a rancher who raised cattle on the land. We had set out to nurture creativity— admittedly a difficult challenge—but judging by the reactions I received from the developers who eventually worked there and from the outpouring of results from their work, we achieved the goal.

Opting Out

After my success with developing the criteria for the research center, I was invited to become part of an executive school for about 10 IBMers considered to have the potential to become high-level executives of the company. (One of my fellow students became the president of IBM, and four others became IBM division presidents. I was the only one of the group to leave the company, looking for a new opportunity at Apple.)

The very elite session was held at one of their executive centers in upstate New York, which we knew as the Guggenheim estate but these days is sometimes referred to as "a former IBM country club."

One function I attended at the estate had major speakers from MIT, Harvard, and Columbia University, plus a lot of outside speakers—people such as Joseph Campbell, who specialized in the use of myths in literature and life, and Barry Commoner, an American biologist, college professor, and eco-socialist, as well as a one-time presidential candidate—a man whom many consider to be the father of today's environmental movement. Another was the author/corporate consultant Peter Drucker, with whom I had had the clash described earlier. Conversations about society's direction and vision were stimulating, and it was a very exciting opportunity to offer ideas and hear them discussed, along with gaining insights into the IBM business and how the company should approach the future.

As the final session of the gathering, the chairman and CEO of IBM, Frank Carey, came in and sat down with us for an open discussion of issues. I brought up my frustration over IBM not moving more toward the consumer market, which every sign showed was going to be a huge opportunity. That's when he gave me the analogy that IBM was like a supertanker, taking a long time to make a change of course. His remark was what made me realize I did not want to be on the crew of a supertanker. It was just sheer dumb luck that I would eventually discover the satisfaction of sailing on a Pirate ship commanded by the greatest corporate Pirate of all time.

The Workplace

One aspect of creating an innovative team is almost always overlooked: providing a suitable space—a unique, distinctive workplace that sets the team apart and reduces the opportunities for interference from The Navy of the larger organization. An appropriate workspace can be critical to creating the innovative culture you are seeking. This is one aspect in which creating a start-up or entrepreneurial organization has an advantage over creating an innovative team within an existing company and its traditional culture: you get to begin fresh, without worrying about interference.

By the time I reached Apple, I had already lived through the challenge of what it's like to create an appropriate working environment for a Pirate team surrounded by The Navy. One of the things that intrigued Steve when we first met was my story of developing the center for innovation at

IBM—the whole concept of space designed to support innovation and creativity for developers.

In addition to providing a separate building for the Macintosh team, Steve came to understand the truth that the design and quality of the team's workspace could have a lot to do with their productivity and success. He carried out the concepts well beyond what we had done as a team, going to extraordinary—in some ways almost laughable—lengths to provide a unique work environment where people would be focused on the product without distraction and would be distinctly separated from the rest of the company. He intuitively understood the key idea: space that promotes innovation is key to the innovative process.

The Mac building became the beginning of Steve's interest in making sure that the facilities would play a role in sparking innovation and in keeping it alive. In the design of the working space, Steve's focus was on making sure every aspect would contribute to enhancing creativity and fostering teamwork. He took into account a lot of the information I provided about what we had done at IBM. In fact, I arranged through an old IBM friend to sneak Steve and me into the Santa Teresa Lab so he could see for himself the features I had been describing.

One curiosity of that visit: Steve had not yet become famous and one of the most widely recognized faces in America. As we moved around the IBM facility, no one recognized Steve, but quite a few people remembered me from my IBM days. Steve was amused that for this one short span of time, I seemed to be more famous than he, the cofounder of a thriving start-up.

For the Apple Mac building, if you could have looked at it from overhead, you would have seen that the interior was designed as for an orchestra, with the leader (Steve) in the front of the building and work areas for the various teams fanned out like sections of the orchestra—the engineering group, then software, graphic design, and the admin group including finance and HR.

A common area offered electronic games and Ping-Pong, a piano, and plenty of snacks. And these weren't just for scheduled break times: they were there to be used whenever any employee felt the impulse or desire.

Among the decorations in this area were some products Steve loved for their design, including a motorcycle of his, a historic BMW bike. The bike and other items were there to remind the Mac team about the importance of great design.

Free food and health drinks were always available. The drinks were from a company called Odwalla, a young California outfit; Steve, who was addicted to eating natural foods—a practice he followed all his adult life—had discovered Odwalla, became a great fan himself, and decided to stock the drink shelves in the Mac building with nothing but. His passion for Odwalla became an item for journalists, which resulted in the company becoming famous.

Of course, there wasn't any need for "dress-down Fridays"—a practice that became popular at many companies, when formal business attire wasn't required on Fridays and it was okay to show up in jeans and casual clothes. Steve was already dressing in what became his standard: a black turtleneck or mock turtleneck, jeans or shorts, and sandals. Almost all Apple employees except for the executives took that as permission to come to work in just about any type of clothing they wanted.

Still, Steve loved to throw TGIF parties—"Thank God It's Friday"—that often included his favorite soul/rhythm-and-blues band.

While few companies are in a position to be so lavish in their workspace arrangements, the facilities for teams you hope will be innovative and creative should be as nurturing as you can afford to make them—the kind of place that has your people looking forward to coming to work each day.

One Infinite Loop

Later, after the Macintosh was released, Steve was able to push the Apple board into a commitment to create a new Apple company headquarters and campus. (Ironically, the property that the company chose to build on was right across the street from the IBM Santa Teresa Labs software development center that I had been responsible for.)

It took a few years, of course, but once the new headquarters buildings at the made-up address of One Infinite Loop in Cupertino were finished and occupied, a few pieces of the old Pirate philosophy spread throughout the whole of Apple Computer. Conference rooms were identified by names sure to bring a smile because they were so anti-corporate and unconventional; names like Da Vinci, Inspiration, and Mission Impossible (after a popular television adventure show of the time). They also included brands of apples: Pippin, Sundance, Fuji, Granny Smith, and so on. Free popcorn was available from popcorn carts scattered throughout the buildings on every floor. Meetings held midday might have catered lunches brought in at company expense, and there were often several of these every day.

The business of the company got done, but it got done in a lighthearted, fun atmosphere that helped keep spirits high.

Other U.S. companies in more recent times have created their own versions of a novel setting to make the work environment a pleasing place to be. At the main offices of Google, known as the Googleplex, there is a playground-like atmosphere, with Astroturf on the floors, and bringing your bike or even your dog to work is okay. Employees don't have to go to a gym; they can just head for one of the workout rooms right on campus, or for one of the swimming pools, or one of several volleyball courts where the games are played on soft beach sand instead of hardwood floors.

In some ways the place has more the feeling of an extraordinarily well-equipped college dorm, or an amusement park, thanks to all of the decorative objects in bright, neon colors. Much of the work is collaborative, often with three people sharing a cubicle. Others work in yurts—large round tents with vertical walls and conical roofs, a design imported from Central Asia and Mongolia.

The company's New York offices, called Google East, are located in a vast, block-long former warehouse building across the street from the famous Chelsea Market. Want to save some time getting to your next meeting? Employees are welcome to use bicycles or skateboards in the hallways. The very large cafeteria offers a wide variety of food, and it's open 24 hours a day. At the far end is an actual ice cream truck that used to roam the streets of New York; choose your flavor, and don't forget to ask for one of their chocolate chip cookies—fresh baked and delicious.

Apple's Space Ship

In June 2011, the city council of Cupertino, California—where Apple has always had its main offices—was scheduled to hold a hearing on the company's request to build a large new corporate campus. Steve was by then quite ill. But still putting a very high premium on the workspace of his innovators, he made the effort to personally present the case for approval of Apple's plans for a massive, futuristic-looking building.

He was helped in from a back door dressed in his trademark black turtleneck and jeans. The bright lights of the room exaggerated how ill he looked, which for people who had known him when he was healthy and vital was especially painful to see. But he had felt the need to be there in person because he had come to believe way back in the Macintosh days how important the workspace is when you want to create an innovative culture.

He came knowing that Apple was the biggest taxpayer in the city, and so wielded a lot of clout, but also knowing that the council would only approve the construction if they were convinced that it was the right thing to do for the community. He knew that without their approval, Apple could not proceed. So Steve began with something of a sales pitch.

Explaining that Apple's existing headquarters held only 2,800 people but that the company had a total of over 12,000 scattered around Silicon Valley, he said, "We're just out of space [but] we've got a plan that lets us stay in Cupertino. As Hewlett-Packard has been shrinking lately they decided to sell [some] property and we bought it. We bought that and we bought some adjacent property that used to [be] apricot orchards, and we've got about 150 acres."

Then he launched into a typical Steve Jobs sales pitch:

We've hired some great architects to work with, some of the best in the world I think, and we've come up with a design that puts 12,000 in one building. Think about that. That's rather odd. 12,000 people in one building. We've seen these office parks with lots of buildings. They get pretty boring, pretty fast. So we'd like to do something better than that. It's a pretty amazing building.

His next bit of description was picked up by most of the reporters who covered the appearance:

It's a little like a spaceship landed. . . . It's a circle. It's curved all the way around.

In case anyone on the council had missed the point, he made it clear:

If you build things, this is not the cheapest way to build something. There is not a straight piece of glass in this building. It's all curved.

In fact, Steve pointed out, for the Apple retail stores around the world, Apple's contractors had developed extraordinary expertise in meeting the company's demands for glass walls:

> We've used our experience making retail buildings all over the world now, and we know how to make the biggest pieces of glass in the world for architectural use. We can make it curve all the way around the building. . . . It's pretty cool.

The former HP campus, Steve told the council, was mostly office space, with only 20 percent of the property landscaped. The new campus, he said, would be *80* percent landscaping, with most of the parking underground.

The focus on being able to work in a beautiful environment, isolated from the city, obviously has Steve's signature all over it. As I heard him explain the design, I couldn't help but remember his preferred way of having one-on-one meetings: during long outdoor walks.

At the end of the presentation, Steve left immediately, with the same assistant helping him and with a guard to ensure his privacy. I felt a sense of joy for him finally having the design for the new campus he had been dreaming of for years, but I also felt great sadness over his condition.

His remarks at the city council session would be the last public appearance he would ever make. He had obviously put out a great personal effort to be there and had made the effort for a cause that meant so much to him and to the continued success of the extraordinary company he had created: a company of innovators, Pirates who in a few years would be sailing in a workspace that would continue to encourage great work.

He knew that this space-age building would be essential for keeping alive Apple's spirit of innovation that he had worked so hard to create. It was like a treasure he was bequeathing to his shipmates.

Steve was to die only four months later.

12

When Selling Becomes More Important than the Product

I didn't see it then, but it turned out that getting fired from Apple was the best thing that could have ever happened to me. The heaviness of being successful was replaced by the lightness of being a beginner again, less sure about everything. It freed me to enter one of the most creative periods of my life.

—Steve Jobs

I n the early days, Steve and I had often talked about how well the Macintosh team was performing because they were focused on a single product. He didn't like the technology decisions being made by the teams developing the new Apple III and Lisa computers, but at least each of the teams was focused on a single product. Steve's dream was that he would eventually see the product-focused team become the standard throughout Apple.

Meanwhile, Steve recognized that the company had achieved amazing success despite never having a CEO with sound credentials for running a company, such as Apple. He set his sights on finding a seasoned business leader who understood consumer marketing. The man he found, John Sculley, certainly fit that description.

If you are familiar with the Apple story, you know that Steve and John at first got along like a pair of long-lost brothers. Journalists wrote about the two that it was as if they were "joined at the hip." They were learning from each other and were each other's greatest admirer. Those glory days lasted some two years.

But Steve had forgotten about his dream of keeping Apple a product-focused company. He had succeeded in picking a leader who understood consumer marketing, but there were two great flaws in his choice. John's marketing expertise was in selling soft drinks, and he knew nothing about technology. Worse, John would never be able to think like a Pirate. His entire working life had been spent in The Navy—naturally enough, since virtually every American company, large and small, was run that way, and even today all but a few still are (think Google, think Facebook).

When John arrived, Apple was already in deep trouble. But of the three innovative development projects, both the Apple III and the Lisa had flopped in the marketplace. With those products folded, there was no longer any innovation going on anywhere at Apple except in the Mac group. The mouse, PostScript, the laser printer—all these new technologies—came out of Mac.

Apple was caught between an old technology, the Apple II, and the new technology, the Mac. But when the Mac had been introduced, it had created a situation that, in hindsight, is laughable—though Steve chose to overlook it at the time. At almost the same time the Mac reached the market, a new Apple II was also introduced: the Apple IIe. Sales of the IIe soared and became the cash cow that was funding all of Apple. The Macintosh—the novel machine that was years ahead and would change the nature of personal computing—was at first a hard sell. In those early months of its existence, lacking software programs, there wasn't really very much a user could do with it. So, initially, Mac sales were slow, very much below what Steve had forecast.

The task John Sculley faced was how to phase out the old products and replace them with the new product, the Mac. At the core of this problem was the ultimate conflict that led to the Jobs-Sculley clash.

Despite the mammoth free publicity from newspapers, magazines, and TV news/interview shows generating excitement about Steve and his new product, months after the Mac had been launched sales were far from what had been projected by the Apple sales organization. Steve wanted to know why. I met with him and discussed what to do. I felt the only way was for him to confront the sales managers in the field and find out for himself why sales weren't better. I knew that he could not challenge the direction that had been set by John Sculley and by marketing VP Bill Campbell without firsthand information. He took me with him on a fact-finding trip to New York, so we could find out from the East Coast sales execs, face-to-face, what was going on. (Steve wanted to hit the East Coast because a majority of Apple sales came from the eastern region of the country.)

We stayed at one of Manhattan's most elegant (and most expensive) hotels, the Carlyle—which Steve liked because John F. Kennedy used to stay there. It was also right across Central Park from Steve's new apartment, still under renovation, next to where John Lennon of the Beatles lived. (Steve once invited actress Diane Keaton, who lived in the same building, to visit him. Curious, she went. She was impressed that the apartment occupied the top three floors of one of the building's towers, but complained afterward that Steve had talked on and on about nothing but technology. The visit did not lead to anything more like a regular date.)

We were in New York to accomplish three things: visit stores selling Apple products, meet the East Coast sales managers, and meet with the software developers who had not yet delivered their promised software programs for the Mac.

First we visited several of the big computer stores. This was when Steve saw the problem for himself: the Mac was a great draw, attracting people who had heard so much about it and wanted to see it for themselves. That part was wonderful. But Steve eavesdropped as people who came in thinking they might buy a Mac were given reasons they would be better off buying a PC—the real reasons being left unspoken: that the store and the sales reps made more money selling PCs than selling Macs.

He and I also saw that most of the sales clerks were poorly trained and were not knowledgeable about what made the Macintosh so superior, so much easier to learn and use. We ran into one sales clerk who didn't even know how to operate a Mac. Steve tried to get him fired but the store manager wasn't going to take orders from someone who didn't pay his salary, even if that someone was Steve Jobs.

While we were in Manhattan having dinner one night and discussing Mac sales, I said no one really knows what the Mac is. I offered to bet Steve $100 that no one in the restaurant could say what a Macintosh was.

He took the bet. Sure enough, our informal poll proved I was right—not a single person knew or admitted to knowing about a computer called Macintosh. (Some said it was a variety of apple, which Steve had to count as a wrong answer.)

Of course, Steve, like John Kennedy, never carried money with him. I never got my $100.

The next part of the trip was to meet with the Apple sales managers for that region to get their stories. They said it was a tough sale because the Macintosh lacked a hard drive, didn't have enough software, and the display wasn't in color. Steve wasn't satisfied by their explanations.

Afterward, I pointed out to him something that struck me during the conversations: the Mac wasn't just competing with Windows machines; it was also competing with our own Apple IIe. The IIe was a major sales success, so hot that the sales reps didn't have to do much to move the product, and they were making very high commissions. The scads of people who loved their Apple II were upgrading en masse to the relatively inexpensive IIe. Why should a rep spend time pushing the harder-to-sell Mac, when getting the stores to sell the IIe was such a dream?

Steve had found some of the answers he was looking for, but nothing he heard offered the possibility of an easy fix.

Understanding All Parts of the Sales Equation

After those meetings, next on the agenda were meetings with the software developers, including Microsoft, as well as some companies that have since faded from the equation, such as Lotus and Aldus. Steve wanted to pressure them about their not coming through yet with their promised software for the Mac. He was not in a good mood over the lack of progress.

I was looking forward to meeting Mitch Kapor, founder of Lotus, because of his unusual background. He had been raised in New York and after studying psychology became a music director and disc jockey at a radio station. He was headed for teaching philosophy at MIT but had been doing some computer programming on the side, which led to his becoming involved in the development of VisiCalc, the first-ever spreadsheet program. It had become an incredible success on the Apple II and is sometimes credited with being the program that turned the personal computer from a hobbyist machine into a useful tool for everyone.

For all its success, VisiCalc was somewhat clumsy and clunky. Two years before the Macintosh was introduced, Mitch left VisiCalc to start his own software company, Lotus, and created a competing program called Lotus 1-2-3, which quickly became the leading spreadsheet software. This was the first bundled package that had a spreadsheet and a database manager in one application, and many today believe this program laid the groundwork for Microsoft Office.

When Mitch showed up at the Carlyle for the meeting, I found him more or less as I had imagined him: in his midfifties and clean shaven, he was casually dressed. He had a reputation of being quite laid back, so I was curious to see how the easy-going Mitch would get along with the out-spoken Steve.

Mitch complained that the Mac operating system software was so poorly done that it was very difficult to write applications for it. He also complained that with the sales volume of the Mac so low, Lotus couldn't afford to spend a lot of time on the new app.

Steve was not happy. He accused Mitch of being swayed by a loyalty to Microsoft and said that by acting out of greed, he was selling off the future. The meeting was as cordial as possible but did not end on a positive note. Steve abruptly stood up and said, "Thanks for coming, Mitch. Goodbye."

A Meeting of Titans

When we got back to Cupertino, Steve's meeting with Bill Gates didn't go any better. Bill flew down and was ushered into the Picasso meeting room. Steve often kept Bill waiting; I was never sure whether Steve wanted to finish what he was in the middle of first, or if keeping Bill waiting was a tactic to put him at a little disadvantage by making him uncomfortable. Or if maybe it was just some little-boy act of Steve's, as a way of saying, "I'm more important than you are."

Steve did not like or respect Bill Gates. At almost every meeting with Bill that I attended, Steve lived up to his reputation for being difficult. At this meeting in Cupertino after our East Coast trip, Steve was openly rude, talking down to Bill—*literally* talking down to him: Steve bounced out of his chair so that Bill had to be looking up at him while Steve spewed in that candid, earnest-but-hurtful way he sometimes used when his emotions were near the surface. Bill made complaints similar to what we had heard from Mitch about the Mac operating system being complex and Mac sales too weak. Steve scolded Bill with a line that became famous: "Bill, you don't get it: Hardware drives software. Software is the glue for the user; the hardware is just what they see."

After Bill left and after Steve had relaxed, I said to him, "Steve, I understand your contempt for Bill, but being rude isn't the answer. The answer is proving you're right."

Good advice, I thought, but it would be more than 20 years before it happened.

It was clear from our trip and the follow-up meetings that the computer stores did not have selling the Mac as a priority and that the outside developers did not have creating software for the Mac as a priority.

Steve was left facing a challenge: the only way the situation was going to change was for the Macintosh to see a major boost in sales. But how?

Choosing the Wrong Direction

What would it take to get more people buying Macs? I tried to push toward getting the consumer message heard with a suggestion that I thought would work brilliantly. The head of U.S. car manufacturer Chrysler at the time was the charismatic Lee Iacocca. When the company hit a hardship period, unable to sell enough cars, Chrysler and its ad agency created a series of television commercials featuring CEO Lee himself. Standing in front of the camera, with one hand on the fender of a Chrysler car, Lee explained the features and reasons why your car choice should be a Chrysler. The ads were compelling enough to bring a turn-around in the fortunes of the company.

If Lee hadn't been such an engaging, outgoing person, the commercials would have been a bad waste of money. But he had just the personality to be able to bring it off.

I argued that Steve was at least as compelling a speaker as Lee—we had all seen that from the session when he first introduced the Macintosh to a large audience of reporters and others, as well as on other occasions. He could talk for a couple of hours at a time and hold an audience riveted.

My idea was to do an ad with Steve standing next to a Mac, explaining the great features of this great product. I thought that ad would be a terrific way to stimulate sales and let the customers know about Steve's compassion for his products.

Steve was more than willing and took the idea to CEO John Sculley. Nothing doing: John shot it down.

Here was another example—I had seen many in my career—of an idea only being considered worthwhile if it came from the sales side of the house. Steve and I sat down with John Sculley and marketing VP Bill Campbell to discuss what major changes could be made to improve the lagging sale of Macs. The decision was that we needed to build an internal sales team to focus on selling to the corporate world. I was instructed to quietly hire 2,000 sales people.

During this time, Steve and I talked a lot about the focus on sales outweighing any focus on the product. Like Steve, I didn't think pushing the Mac to corporate America instead of to the consumer was wise. At the same time, almost no advertising was being done, so the messages about the groundbreaking features of the Mac were not being heard.

For those who don't know or have forgotten, on other personal computers at the time, the way you told the computer to write a file to the floppy drive required typing out a command, letter by letter, that went something like:

copy c:/Letters/LtrToJohnApr12.doc d:/JohnFiles/

On the Macintosh, of course, you only needed to drag the icon for the file to the icon for the JohnFiles folder in the list of files on the floppy

To copy a whole directory, you would (if you had managed to commit the various commands to memory) type something like:

xcopy -e c:/Letters d:/Letters

But the explanations of how phenomenally easier it was to learn and to use the Mac were not being heard.

And instead of spending money to get that message out, I was under orders to hire 2,000 sales people to knock on doors of IT managers in corporations that had been buying their computers from IBM for years and weren't likely to pay much attention to a sales person from a start-up computer company.

The first thing that entered my mind was how in the Army I was sent to boot camp, which had exactly the same kind of goal: training in the needed skills but also converting recruits to a new mind-set. So, why not have a Sales Boot Camp? We found an abandoned school and an ex-Marine drill sergeant.

The challenge was to hire those 2,000 sales people but not let our distributors know what we were doing. We had to recruit all over the United States but keep the effort quiet. This was one time when we made an exception: We couldn't handle that huge effort in-house, so we put the job in the hands of several recruiting firms, with instructions that they post blind ads and not tell the applicants the name of the company.

We had a tough educational process through hiring outside recruiters. We had to convey to the recruiters what a Pirate is and what an A-player is, and then make sure we had done a good enough job that they would really adhere to your standards. To do this right is no small challenge, but we found it's possible to do if you're sufficiently committed to the effort.

Then we had to bring all the new recruits to Cupertino for orientation. Obviously they had to become experts in all aspects of using the Apple products. Less obvious but just as important was bringing every one of them up to speed on the Apple culture, because people would be judging the company by how the sales reps explained, spoke, and behaved.

We monitored very carefully every step of the way, making sure each recruit was, despite the military atmosphere, becoming truly attuned to the Apple culture. *Attitude* counted more than textbook knowledge. We felt very confident about those who made it through.

And we were in business. The course turned our recruits into sales reps who were totally immersed in the Apple Way, completely product oriented, and ready to hit the street selling.

But while the recruiting and culture-training efforts were successful, the program would later backfire. It was the beginning of the end for Apple's product-driven Pirate culture.

In preparation for the major sales conference in Hawaii, when that new 2,000-person sales force would be introduced to the Macintosh, each of the VPs was asked to make a presentation about their part of Apple, along with any information that could help the new sales recruits understand the company and its culture.

I put together a presentation that included a videotape assembled from footage and still photos that captured the heart and soul of the Apple culture, the people, and how we worked together.

At the end of my speech and the video, I got a standing ovation from the audience. When I walked off the stage, Steve Jobs was standing in the wings. Offended by an item in the video that included him, he growled at me, "Jay, that was the worst presentation I ever saw."

What a come-down from the standing ovation. And regardless of what had annoyed him, the attack was overboard. After I caught my breath, I said, "Steve, I have two words for you: f__k you."

I walked away. About 20 yards further on, I encountered John Sculley. He said, "Jay, that was terrific." Nice, but it didn't ease the pain I was feeling from Steve's comments.

My five staff members who had helped me put this together had heard all this and were devastated. I ordered a tour guide and a limo filled with food and drink, and took my staff off for a fun day on Oahu for the celebration I felt they deserved. We toured, swam, surfed, snorkeled, ate, drank, and had a great day.

At the end of the day I was asked, "Who do we charge this to?" I said, "Steve Jobs."

When we got back, I received a call from Apple's accounting department asking what this charge was for. I said, "It was Steve's way of rewarding us for the great job we did at the sales meeting." The lady said, "Okay."

The final installment of the incident didn't come for another couple of weeks. Steve and I were meeting to talk about bonuses for the Mac management. As we sat down, Steve said, "Jay, I have two words for you: I'm sorry."

His apology meant a great deal to me, especially since it was one of the only times I remember him ever apologizing to anyone for anything.

It had been the only time in our countless debates, arguments, and disagreements that Steve really got to me in a way I have never forgotten.

But Steve's blowup at me was far from the worst friction of that sales meeting. It was there that the Jobs-Sculley conflict over Mac sales came to a head, with a confrontation between the two, in front of other people, that was worse than anything you see on reality television.

Leaving Hawaii to come home from the meeting, Steve changed his flight so he would not be on the same plane as John. A week later, Steve made a comment in his Monday meeting, in front of his staff, criticizing John for the problems in Mac sales.

I pulled Steve out of the meeting and told him, "You and John need to resolve your issues—we can't have the chairman of the board and the president of the company engaged in open warfare." I saw only one solution that was good for Apple, a solution only Steve, as chairman of the board, could make happen. "Walk over to John's office," I said, "and tell him he's out!"

He wouldn't do it. This was the first time I saw Steve in an avoidance posture. For some reason I've never understood, he did not want to confront John. And, ironically, John didn't want to confront him.

I set up an evening meeting for the three of us in Steve's office. (In his biography of Steve, Walter Isaacson says John grabbed me as a witness and went to confront Steve. That's not at all what happened. I was the one who set up the meeting, I controlled it, and at this point there wasn't any confronting.) Steve started in about changing the whole company into a Mac-style organization, product focused and moving toward the new technology. John strongly defended the current Apple organization.

To my surprise and shock, Steve started to sob because of what he saw as John's incompetence. "You don't get it! You're ruining Apple and the Mac!" Steve choked out between sobs.

John got up abruptly and walked out. I was left there with this sobbing chairman, wondering what would come next. But what passed through my mind was that he had just given John ammunition to say Steve was unstable. The only previous time I had seen Steve well up in tears was when he was telling me late one night about a failed relationship with a woman he really loved.

At a meeting of the executive staff, Steve confronted John, insisting he was the wrong person to be running Apple. John was stunned. He knew Steve had started gathering forces to try to push him out of the company and replace him as CEO. And now Steve was attacking him in front of the top people of the company. Stunned, John announced he wanted each person to say whether he supported John in continuing to run the company. It was an emotional moment for everyone present. Most spoke about how much they admired Steve; some even said how much they loved him. But each in turn then said he wanted John to continue running the company.

I was the one lone voice for Steve. (This was another miscue in the Isaacson book: He makes it sound as if no one in the room spoke up to insist that Steve, not John, should be running the company.) I knew how difficult he could be, but I also knew that he had a vision of what Apple could be and a vision of where computer technology was headed. John had neither. I said that the company needed Steve in charge, that the company's survival depended on it.

But the consensus ruled.

I want to clear the record about what happened next. The board of directors, under pressure, came to recognize the need to look into the facts about Steve as the leader of the Macintosh group. The board appointed two of its members to quietly interview people in the Mac group and others around Apple who had direct contact with Steve. Based on that report, which included details of Steve's frequently abrasive, verbally abusive behavior, the board voted to remove Steve from his position in charge of the Macintosh group and give him another assignment—one that would not involve being in charge of a specific team.

When Apple CEO John Sculley sat down with Steve to discuss the decision with him, Steve was so was upset at being told that his Macintosh group was being taken away from him that he got up and walked out.

Although he would always refer to it afterward as his having been fired, that wasn't what really happened. Still, here was a situation where the cofounder of the company was being removed from leading the team he had headed through the creation of a ground-breaking product; to me, that's equivalent to being fired, even though he was being offered a different position.

Steve called me about 2 AM that morning, again sobbing. He said that he had lost his company and now he would be on the sideline of the great Mac revolution. He said he was going to leave for Europe and might decide to spend time as a world traveler. The unspoken message was that he was angry or humiliated or both, and he didn't want to stick around to be hounded by reporters and embarrassed by questions of the Macintosh team members.

I told him, "Steve, without you, Sculley and Apple are now on the sideline." During that phone call, I decided to speak with the board members, one by one, hoping I could convince them to give their support to Steve and terminate John's contract.

A few days later, after all my (fruitless) meetings with the board members, Steve called me and invited me to lunch at his home in Woodside. He served up a pleasant meal—vegetarian, of course—and then we took a walk around the grounds. With his boyish enthusiasm, he said, "I can't believe you stood up to Sculley and then went around him to the board."

Then, again, the tears began flow. He said, "No one else at Apple really cares. Thank you for standing up for me."

I said, "Steve, I really want Apple to succeed, and I think it will with you. But without you, I believe they'll eventually fail." I went on to say that he needed to make amends with the board and change his leadership style.

His response was painful and misguided. "Thanks," he said. "I think what you've done will change the minds of the board." But I had already told him the responses I had gotten ranged from negative to noncommittal. Not a single person had held out any real hope of a vote for Steve.

As I was leaving, he said, "Jay, I know you have put yourself in harm's way with Sculley."

"Sometimes that's what happens when you stand up for your principles," I answered.

Steve had stood up for his, as well. Now the door was shut to him at the company he had cofounded. He would take no active role in managing the company or developing its products until the turn of fate that brought him back. He would launch NeXT and would buy the computer graphics group that became Pixar, but he would have no direct connection with Apple for the next 12 years.

Apple Becomes The Navy

Throughout its history until the day Steve left, Apple had been a company organized around product groups—highly independent economic profit centers that operated almost like stand-alone companies.

With Steve gone, John Sculley didn't waste any time reorganizing Apple according to the way that The Navy companies are always organized. His mantra was captured by an old business adage, "Expect what you inspect." His approach was about control.

In almost any other company in the world, John's approach might have been a rousing success. But Steve knew that at Apple, only a culture organized around *product* groups would be successful. Once Apple was reorganized to become a traditional function-oriented organization, John and the two CEOs who followed him presided over a company that had run off its tracks. The magic was gone.

Months after Steve had left the company, Apple had to lay off over 1,300 employees, shut down four manufacturing facilities, and reorganize to focus on improving and marketing the Macintosh. If Steve's vision for the company had been listened to, all of that hardship, all of those setbacks, could have been avoided.

Another of the CEOs went a big step further in organizing the company by functions, with only a few high-level executives reporting directly to the CEO. As a result, there was even less connection between the leaders and the product. The people who should have been giving product guidance were just administering a plan. The company lost its product focus, concentrating on programs and software updates instead of on making killer products.

The Loudest Voices: Sales and Marketing

Steve later griped to me about organizational priorities, broad issues, and business in general but it was obvious that the conversation was really about Apple.

Why does one company after another turn out mediocre products? Steve understood that the sales staff brings in the money. But when Apple started being ruled over by a leader whose sole expertise was in sales and marketing, Apple's corporate thinking changed completely. Corporate priorities and the communication of ideas became centered on how to move product into the hands of the buyer. Executive meetings dwelt on revenues, profit and loss, and stock price performance, rather than on the features and the excellence of the product.

In fact one decision that was totally rejected by the Mac Pirates was not sticking with the original goal of selling the Mac for $999. The decision to make the selling price $2,495 was based on providing a fat marketing budget.

Decisions like that, made over and over at Apple to the point of nearly scuttling the company, weren't unique. Companies continue to make that same mistake.

Only when the product is truly superior—hopefully so superior that the product sells itself—do the sales and marketing people take a back seat to product development.

That's a mistake. The mantra must become, "The product is king."

Sales Focus versus Product Focus at IBM

I had seen the problem of the sales force controlling company decisions while I was working at IBM. I told the story to Steve, in hopes of making him speak out more forcefully to the Apple decision-makers.

Sales was the real power behind IBM's success and had been the driving force since Tom Watson Sr. became the company's first CEO. I illustrated the fact to Steve by telling him the story of a run-in I had with the man who was the IBM head of sales, John Akers, when I was manager of a company unit in California.

John went to the IBM executive committee and recommended that I accept the transfer of 200 programmers from Manhattan—people who were on the rolls of the sales department but, John said, were not needed in sales.

I visited the Manhattan facility, talked to a number of the programmers, and found that none of them wanted to move to California, and especially not to the part of California where my unit was located, an area the programmers considered a "cultural wasteland." It was clear to me John's plan would not work.

However, he convinced the executive committee, and I was told to make it happen. After a struggle and many concessions, we got about half of them to come to California; the rest quit and left the company.

After the crew from Manhattan had gotten settled in, one of the New York programmers came to me with the suggestion that we try the idea called vanpooling. IBM would buy some vans—vehicles that could hold a driver and seven passengers. For each van, one employee would accept responsibility for finding seven others to ride with him each day; he'd keep the van at his own home and the eight of them would split the gas charges.

This would save money for the employees who had to commute, plus help the environment by having fewer cars on the road. It was a great idea that had special appeal for the new employees who had come in from New York.

The idea had to get corporate blessing. I flew back to IBM headquarters and made the pitch. I was told the idea was so novel that it would require approval of all the division heads and would have to be approved, as well, by the board of directors. John Akers was one of those who had to approve. He reluctantly agreed it was a good idea and gave his half-baked approval.

I would find out in time that John was only agreeing because he thought it would give him leverage in getting approval for an idea he had been pushing for years without success. He wanted IBM to lease a car for every one of the IBM salespeople.

At a meeting of the board and the division heads, I made my presentation, and the division heads were asked to indicate whether they have any problems with the vanpooling proposal. John spoke up and said, "I'll give my approval to this, provided the board will approve giving sales people leased cars."

He was asking the company to lease a car for each person in a sales force of over 150,000 people; the economics were staggering. I wasn't surprised when the board refused to agree to John's proposal. The result was that John in turn refused to go along with the vanpooling proposal, and because of him, it was shot down.

Once again, sales had ruled a corporate decision.

I was shocked when, a few years later, John Akers became IBM's CEO. Then, in 1988, John announced a sweeping restructuring of IBM. He created five new highly autonomous organizations that were to be responsible for the company's innovation, design, and manufacturing. These moves were intended to decentralize the company and give significantly more responsibility to a younger generation of mangers. The new divisions were affectionately called the Baby Blues, a play on a journalist's nickname for IBM, Baby Blue.

The company's performance continued to decline.

In 1992 IBM faced its first losing quarter in its 100 years. But I wasn't surprised that under John Akers, the company went into a steep decline and he eventually became the only CEO in IBM's history to reign over the company losing money, posting a loss of $5 billion, at the time the largest loss by any American corporation in history.

The old sales tricks did not work anymore, and all the IBM executives were from the sales side, not products or operations. Most of the good product people had left the company.

It was a painful illustration of what happens to a company that does not have vision or that has a CEO who does not understand the true direction of the market.

When John Akers left the post, CNBC named him as one of the "Worst American CEOs of All Time," stating, "While the rest of the world was moving toward personal computing, Akers remained stuck in the mainframe age, never quite figuring out what to do."[1] IBM was paralyzed by lack of direction. As I put it when I left IBM, "You need to get out of the computer room!" When I spoke about all this to Steve Jobs, reminding him of remarks John Sculley had made as CEO, Steve answered, "Yes, he was a smart, fantastic salesperson, but he didn't know anything about product. It's the product, stupid!"

Enter Louis Gerstner as IBM's replacement CEO, a proven operational executive from American Express who had been credited with the expansion of new users for the card. In evaluating the product, Gerstner found out that most retail stores did not accept American Express cards, nor did airlines. He saw that corporations, which persuaded to issue the cards could be provided a better tracking system for business expenses. So, although not a technical guy, he understood the value of a product and of user satisfaction.

Louis Gerstner not only had to take over a losing business but had to reshape the culture out of the old IBM ways. Incidentally, it had been reported that two other people were approached before Gerstner: Bill Gates and John Sculley. Either of those choices would have been very interesting to watch.

Gerstner decided IBM needed to become a more broad-based information technology integrator that could help its clients move into the new age of computing and give its customers complete IT solutions. Does this sound familiar? Steve had to take the same type of steps to turn around Apple after what I might call his second coming.

The turnaround worked for IBM, and the CEOs who followed have been very product focused. One of them, Sam Palmisano, who took over in 2002, introduced a new strategy involving a hub of information that would shift to services and software, often delivered over the Internet from data centers and connecting with all types of devices, including the PC. It is the approach that has come to be called the cloud and is, of course, the new big movement in technology.

In October 2011, while I was in the process of writing this book, IBM named a new CEO, Virginia Romety, another operational, product person. When asked by a *Fortune* magazine writer what her priorities were, her reply included continuing to build on the company's product roadmap.

Clearly, she's someone who gets it—a leader in the Steve Jobs model.

If IBM had had a CEO of that mind-set when I was working there, I would probably never have left.

To date, IBM has had five Nobel Prize winners and the company is now introducing new products—now mostly software—almost on a monthly basis.

The IBM story provides a great lesson in how a company can completely change direction, become product driven, and make a stunning comeback. At the core of that comeback were the IBM Pirates in the development labs who were committed to creating great new technology for the users.

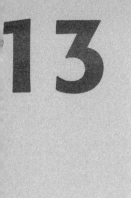

13 "And One More Thing"

Looking into the Distance

We don't know where it will lead. We just know there's something much bigger than any of us here.

—Steve Jobs

Once while Steve and I were traveling from New York to Washington, D.C., during a relaxed moment we fell into a discussion of what might become the next bold user interface. I said I was sure it would be voice recognition. Steve thought that was too bold, too far away for the current state of technology. It had to be a handheld device (this was before PDAs had become popular), though he wasn't sure people would adapt to a small screen.

He was wrong about the reluctance to accept a small screen, of course, but his concept about handheld devices has driven Apple for 30 years.

Your ideas need to be bold. Never fear to set a concept as grand as "We are going to change the world with _____." Yet at the same time, the statement of that concept needs to be simple. An example is the digital hub—which Steve first began talking about in 1985. He was already starting to envision all of a user's electronic information being available to all of her digital devices, with the Macintosh as the key device at the center of this hub.

Think about Christopher Columbus setting off from Spain to sail across the Atlantic. He was pursuing a personal conviction that there was land on the other side of the vast, unknown ocean and that he could reach it. When my ancestors crossed the United States in covered wagons, their goal was to bring milk products to the West Coast of America. Bringing their goal to reality meant they had to herd some 50 bulls and cows across the breadth of the continent, settle on their new homesteading land, cut down redwood trees to build homes and barns (those original buildings are now preserved as historical monuments, open to the public), and build the business from the ground up. They hauled milk and cheese products every day to San Francisco.

When the California gold rush started in 1849, it brought an unexpected happy boom to their business. For the inaugural celebration of President Abraham Lincoln in 1861, they produced what was then the world's largest cheese and transported it to Washington for the celebration.

Much of history is the story of bold ideas (though, I admit, not often involving cows). Think of what has triggered over 30 years of innovation from Steve Jobs based on those simple visits to Xerox PARC. The brilliant part of Steve's concept was that it involved how the user interacts with the devices that provide the content they want to use.

Defining the Goal

One day Steve had lunch with a young entrepreneur who had been referred to him by a student Steve had met at one of his Stanford MBA classes. The youngster had been talking to leaders of high-tech companies, seeking a better understanding of what it meant to set a long-term goal. As Steve related this to me afterward, the young man had met with some people at personal-computer maker Tandy Computers, who explained their goal by saying it was to have a Tandy computer on everyone's Christmas wish list.

He then visited another company in the personal-computer business, Commodore, which in those days was a major rival of Apple. He was told that their goal was to see what sounded like a very modest rise in the share price of the company's stock.

This didn't surprise Steve, who held a low opinion of Jack Tramiel, the man who had founded Commodore. Steve considered him a cut-throat entrepreneur who was in the computer business only for the money. After Jack left Commodore, he became head of another personal-computer company, Atari, where they produced a Mac look-alike that came to be dubbed the Jackintosh.

(I was with Steve at the annual Consumer Electronics Show when we ran into Jack, after he had put out the Jackintosh. Steve told him, "Your product is a knock-off and you will never be successful." Jack pulled back his sleeve and showed us a concentration-camp tattoo on his wrist; he told Steve, "I will always be successful. No one can stop me." I had never seen Steve stunned and at a loss for words. He simply turned and walked away, I assume out of embarrassment. I was embarrassed, as well, by Steve's remark to a man who had managed to live through the concentration-camp experience and had risen to become a major businessman.)

Still, a company where the employee focus wasn't on making the best damn products they could but rather simply increasing the stock price was a company that Steve could never have respect for.

By the time the young man doing this research had reached Apple, he already had two answers to his question about the company goal for the personal computer. When he asked Steve, what he got in reply with not a simple statement. Instead, Steve launched into his mode of magical story-telling, talking about "how personal computers are going to change the world." He outlined how the computer would change everything about the way we work, educate our children, and entertain ourselves. This was a grand conception that any thinking person could buy into.

Everyone—or at least everyone who cares about the work they do—wants to buy into a big, grand concept. That's the power of the total concept that Steve was all about. As if he had been holding out for one last hurrah, the day before Steve died, Apple introduced an impressive upgrade: the iPhone 4S. This product contains the ultimate user interface—voice recognition—supported by artificial intelligence. It was one more stepping-stone in achieving the grand view that Steve had always driven for.

The Whole Product

After his Xerox PARC experience, Steve realized that he had to wrestle technology out of hands of the technologists. The conception of the whole product had to grow out of the close understanding of the user by focusing on the user interface.

Up until Steve returned to Apple, the idea of a whole product was all but forgotten, and to me the best example of that is the difference in marketing the operating systems: When you bought an Apple computer, the operating system was part of the package. When you bought a PC, you had to pay extra for the then-current version of Windows—which may account for as much as 30 percent of the sales price of the computer. I always remembered that Microsoft dominated the PC market as an *add-on* product.

As I've noted, Steve soon after his return recognized the talent of the man who was already heading the Apple design team: Jonathon Ive (now addressed as *Sir* Jonathon when he's in the United Kingdom—he was knighted by the Queen in early 2012 in recognition of his design achievements).

Jony shared Steve's mantra of the whole product vision, both the external design—how it looked—and how it worked. Steve wanted the new Macs to lay the groundwork for a design that would be compelling to users. Though the outward appearance went through many iterations, the final bold version set the new iMacs in striking candy-colored translucent plastic cases.

What is especially notable about this decision is that it was made at a time of falling prices in the computer market, and those eye-catching, handsome cases were quite expensive to produce. Jony said about this design approach, "Victories from sales are very short-lived, victories from things you've really worked hard at can have a lasting impact."

And, "Any item designed as a total product holds the possibility of having a lasting impact."

Missteps

Companies that are not focused on their customers, or that lose this focus, can get in trouble quickly. A couple of prime examples took place around the time I was writing this book—instances when users of the company's offerings quickly decided that the offerings had not been well thought out. In both cases, the issues had to do with the overall product and how it was being used. One of these companies was Netflix, which had quickly become a huge success by offering to have a DVD reach you in two days or less, which you could then keep as long as you wanted, with no late fees.

This was a great deal for consumers but a tough challenge for long-established Blockbuster, with local stores in neighborhoods all across the United States. In fact, for Blockbuster, the delinquency fees accounted for a startling amount of money, about 40 percent of overall revenues. So the Netflix concept of no delinquency fees sounded golden.

But after a few years, Netflix decided on a new strategy that represented the company turning its back on its customers. The company announced that it was splitting its operation into two separate parts by creating a new entity, Qwikster. The new structure, it said, would enable the company to focus on providing streaming content—downloading movies directly over the Internet to your home—to replace the less profitable DVD-by-mail service. Customers who wanted both streaming and DVD rental, for games as well as movies and TV shows, would have to have separate accounts at Netflix and Qwikster. The public outcry came so quickly and was so strong that the company finally woke up, canceling the Qwikster concept some three weeks after it was announced. But many previously satisfied customers had soured in their views toward the company, and Netflix stock shares lost a stunning 50 percent of their value.

Also around the same time, one of America's most respected financial institutions, Bank of America, stumbled badly in a similar way. The bank announced that holders of its debit cards would soon see a $5 charge for any month in which they used their card. The announcement triggered what *BusinessWeek* magazine termed "an uproar and threatened exodus by customers."[1] We don't often hear about children's nannies becoming protest organizers, but one 22-year-old nanny started an online petition to the bank, which generated a near-unbelievable level of response and turned out to be one of the pressure points leading to the bank's decision a month later to cancel the new fee, before it had even gone into effect.

I at least give Bank of America credit for listening to the public outcry. Yet if these two organizations had paid better attention to Steve's emphasis on making customer loyalty a top priority, neither of them would have been forced into the position of having to make a very public and very embarrassing back-down.

Incidentally, both of these stories make clear that the whole product concept applies to most service organizations as well as to product companies.

Self-Training

Every product person should be playing with products—working with them, examining, scrutinizing, trying to discover what's unique, what's especially appealing, what's done well, and what's done badly. Hands-on experience is the key to advancing your product sensibility.

Look not just at competitive products but at other products in your life. That new coffee maker: How easy is it to open the box? To use it the first time? To understand the user options and choices?

The same applies to Internet sites. Recently, I signed in to a legal site to create a new will and trust. On this site, the sequence of steps was amazingly easy to figure out; the entire process was seamless. As soon as I was finished, I called on my lead product guy to take a look at the site, and told him to make sure our own site had product instructions that met the same high standard for ease of use.

Content Is King, Platform Is God

The major difference between Apple and other technology companies like Google or Microsoft is that Apple provides both content and the platform to run it on—just think iTunes and how seamlessly it works with the iPod, iPad, and iPhone. In contrast, Google sells advertising and considers that to be content.

One area that Steve could applaud Bill Gates for was Bill's early vision on the crucial value of content. As long ago as early 1996, Bill wrote a perceptive article with a title that has just about become part of the language: "Content is King." The article begins with a prediction that could not have been more accurate: "Content is where I expect much of the real money will be made on the Internet, just as it was in broadcasting."[2]

For once I can say hurray for Bill Gates!

The essay went on to point out that the Internet is the multimedia equivalent of the photocopier, allowing material to be duplicated at low cost, no matter the size of the audience. It also allows information to be distributed worldwide at basically zero marginal cost to the publisher.

As accurate as his crystal ball was all those years ago, Bill included a statement that could only be called laughable from Steve's perspective. "At Microsoft," Gates wrote, "we consider our software to be the content."

Power of the Family—
No User Left Behind

The NeXT software that Apple acquired with the purchase of Steve's company provided the engine for all of Apple's future product development. It became the glue that holds together all the Apple devices as a family—which meets the textbook definition of a product family as a grouping of products whose similarity in resource usage, design, and manufacturing processes facilitates planning on a combined basis.

When Steve left Apple, one of the people he brought along to NeXT was Rich Page, who had been chief designer of the next-generation Macintosh. Rich had been one of the four Apple Fellows, a recognition given to contributors who have played an especially valuable role in developing Apple technology. He was responsible for developing tools, including compilers and hardware, for the first prototyped portable—the color Mac.

His contributions at NeXT included what's called product line engineering, or domain engineering, which refers to product lines that are based on common software, reworked for each product as needed.

Going against the Grain

With Apple, the real revolution began with iTunes, which brought a total rewriting of the rules of the music industry. The new era gave Apple an unprecedented degree of control in setting policy, pricing, and how the profits would be divided up. The record companies begrudgingly acquiesced to Steve's demands.

Steve's success in the face of the entrenched music industry is a lesson for all of us: never be afraid to go against the grain. When Apple launched the iPod, downloading music to a digital platform was considered dead. Sure, there was plenty of that going on, but it was illegal, and the artists and music companies were not seeing any income from it. The music industry was reeling from the pirated music, until Steve came up with his against-the-grain solution.

He went against the grain with the iPad, as well. The tablet market was dead in the water, with PC manufacturers scrambling to find a solution that would draw purchasers. Steve introduced a product very significantly more expensive than other tablets—and you know what happened. The iPad redefined the category. As of this writing, in early 2012, the product has been on the market for less than a year and has sold some 25 million units.

Now it's becoming clear that the iPad is putting the desktop PC market at risk. The iPad is being accepted as a tool by IT departments, opening a totally new market opportunity for Apple.

My mind turns back to several years ago when I would attend client meetings in New York and find the room dominated by BlackBerry phones, while I was the only person with an iPhone. Later, for a time, these meetings were dominated by a lot of the people with both a BlackBerry and an iPhone. But by now pretty much everybody sits down at the table with an iPhone—a major market shift.

How Steve would have enjoyed seeing that.

Staying the Course

On top of all Steve achieved in his lifetime, I believe the visionary Steve Jobs left a roadmap for at least the next three years from the time of his death in late 2011. Setting the pattern for any other company or team that loses its visionary leader, Apple needs to stay fiercely loyal to the strategic ideas that Steve infused into the lifeblood of the company.

Almost as if it had been planned by a benevolent God, the Apple product introduction on the day before Steve died offered a feature new to Apple, with far-reaching impact. Siri, the speak-to-your-phone voice technology incorporated into the iPhone 4S, wasn't first-of-a-kind. Android and other phones had offered their own version of the technology a couple of years earlier. Steve never aimed at being the first; he aimed at getting it right.

Siri is only the starting gate. I believe voice technology is going to be another major game-changer. It will be invoked in every sort of interaction between a human and a machine, from eliminating that pesky remote control in our living rooms, to controlling factories, and even to operating our cars.

When the iPhone 4S was introduced, it received all the attention. Introduced at the same time was iCloud, for remote storage of files and applications, which went virtually unnoticed. Yet iCloud and one element of the iPhone represented the next three to four years of amazing user interface. Today we're still in the keyboard world, while these products were a step toward Steve's vision of the next upgrade to user interface. Subsequent iPhones will offer improved voice recognition, eventually able to understand any e-mail address, street address, web address, message text, application calls, or anything else that you now use the on-screen keyboard for.

With the iCloud, all your data, and possibly your applications as well, are automatically backed up at a remote location on massive server farms where storage for users is unlimited. This means the files you need are always available to whatever computer you're using, at any location around the world where there is an Internet connection. And with never any concern about having compatible apps for the work you're doing.

In addition, with Siri you can also bring files from the cloud to your iPhone.

Steve's vision about changing the world is embodied in these products.

This takes me to the next stop on the vision journey—iTV, Apple's long-awaited television. I believe the handwriting is on the wall: iTV will incorporate not just magnificent images and great sound but, in time if not a feature of the first release, intelligent voice control. And beyond that, I think there is an even bigger play for Apple: involvement of cable and satellite TV using the Apple ecosystem of iCloud and apps, combined with their family of products—iPad, iPhone, and the soon-to-arrive iTV—makes all the sense in the world; it's the ultimate use of content.

Shortly before Steve's death, a man sometimes identified as a Silicon Valley futurist, Paul Saffo, offered this insight: "Apple has beautiful artifacts, but what Steve Jobs has been building is a company whose legacy is ideas."[3] Steve's ideas are the foundation for what some have called the Apple ecosystem, referring to the way his influence is reshaping how the entire industry operates.

While it's impossible to project with confidence the future of your products, what's important is that you be certain your company *will* be part of the future. The simple question is, Are you in this for the long run? If you are, then you need to keep seeking information from personal experiences, relevant news, pundit predictions, and keep asking yourself, *Where is this all going?*

I remember riding on a train with Steve after the Macintosh had been launched. He said, "Jay, I finally feel relaxed. The Mac is out, it's great. And now I can relax a bit."

"Wrong," I said. "The journey has just begun. The hard part is ahead of us."

Coming up with a product is the easy part. What's really hard is to keep a vision going and keep matching the right product to it.

The most critical element in all of this, however, is the user. The two questions you always have to ask yourself are, *Do I really love this product as a user?* and *Will anyone else love it?*

A scene that for me captured the essence of the products Steve Jobs gave us: I was in a restaurant recently and observed a family at a table near me. The daughter, age about 5, was using an iPad. Nearby, at the bar, a 50-something man was also using his iPad.

If your products can come even close to matching this, your vision is the ultimate reality!

14 Flowers at His Doorstep

The Heritage of Steve Jobs

It's not just a job, it's a journey. Let's never forget that. . . . Your customers dream of a happier and better life. Don't move products. Instead, enrich lives.

—Steve Jobs

In his bestselling biography of Steve, Walter Isaacson, in my opinion, looks too much at the negative side of the man, without really understanding the artist side. Isaccson, like other outsiders, paints Steve as "incorrigible, bullying, belittling, and lying." What he misses is that Steve the Artist was getting 150 percent out of people. And though many at Apple felt the humiliating sting of his wrath, very few left because of it. They stayed because it was such a uniquely gratifying place to work. Who wouldn't want to know he had had a hand in creating the iPad, the iPhone, or iTelevision?

The big difference between Steve and other corporate executives is that Steve was like a rock star. He had instant success, lots of money, and was riding high on his fame for being the darling of Silicon Valley. What Steve did not have was a grounding in business or education. His social skills were not what most high-flying executives are expected to possess. When he was starting out, his résumé would not have landed him a job at General Electric or Olivetti, Ford or Gucci. His management style was not the stuff of university textbooks. He wasn't known for his consultative or consensus-building approach.

Instead, he was a *product* artist, a man who related to other artists—musicians in particular—but not to most corporate executives. This was his magic or his curse, however you choose to look at it.

In understanding Steve's leadership qualities, we have to compare him to an impresario or artistic director of a world-class opera company. He was a transformational leader.

A Warning from Steve about Pursuing the Wrong Values

His attitudes about money contributed mightily to his personal distress over what became of Apple in the years he was out of the company. In 1995, while he was away from Apple running his competing start-up company NeXT, Steve sat down for an oral history interview for the Smithsonian Institution. His comments in the interview shed some fascinating light on his values, and provide a warning to all entrepreneurs and business leaders. Talking about what was going on while he was not at Apple, he said,

> What ruined Apple was values . . . bringing a set of values to the top of Apple which were corrupt and corrupted some of the top people who were there, drove out some of the ones who were not corruptible, and brought in more corrupt ones and paid themselves collectively tens of millions of dollars and cared more about their own glory and wealth than they did about what built Apple in the first place—which was making great computers for people to use.
>
> They didn't care about that any more. They didn't have a clue about how to do it and they didn't take any time to find out because that's not what they cared about. They cared about making a lot of money.
>
> So they had this wonderful thing that a lot of brilliant people made called the Macintosh and they got very greedy. And instead

of following the trajectory of the original vision—which was to make this thing an *appliance*, to get this out there to as many people as possible—they went for profits and they made outlandish profits for about four years. Apple was one of the most profitable companies in America for about four years.

What that cost them was the future.

What they should have been doing was making reasonable profits and going for market share, which was what we always tried to do. Macintosh would have had a thirty-three percent market share right now, maybe even higher. . . . Now it's got a single-digit market share and falling. There's no way to ever get that moment in time back.

Of course he couldn't envision that a strange turn of events would take him back to Apple, in position to alter the course of the company and the acceptance of the Macintosh. Based on what he was seeing at the time of the interview, he went on:

The Macintosh will die in another few years and it's really sad. The problem is this: No one at Apple has a clue as to how to create the next Macintosh because no one running any part of Apple was there when the Macintosh was made—or any other product at Apple. They've just been living off that one thing now for over a decade. . . .

It's kind of tragic, but as unemotionally as I can be, that's what's happening. Unless somebody pulls a rabbit out of a hat.

Steve, of course, would himself turn out to be the magician pulling that rabbit out of the hat.

Companies tend to have long glide slopes because of the installed bases. But Apple is just gliding down this slope and they're losing market share every year. Things start to spiral down once you get under a certain threshold.

Apple could have lived forever and kept shipping great products forever. Apple was for a while like Sony. It was the place that made the coolest stuff.

It's Too Easy to Be Satisfied with the Status Quo

In that same Smithsonian conversation mentioned earlier, Steve also addressed other critical reasons why established companies don't perform as well as they could, and why that will always create an opportunity for entrepreneurs and start-up companies.

> One of the things that happens in organizations as well as with people is that they settle into ways of looking at the world and become satisfied with things. And the world changes and keeps evolving and new potential arises but these people who are settled in don't see it.
>
> That's what gives start-up companies their greatest advantage. The sedentary point of view is that of most large companies.
>
> In addition to that, large companies don't usually have efficient communication paths—from the people closest to some of these changes at the bottom of the company to the top of the company, the people making the big decisions.
>
> There may be people at lower levels of the company that see these changes coming but by the time the word ripples up to the highest levels where they can do something about it, it sometimes takes ten years. Even in the case where part of the company does the right thing at the lower levels, usually the upper levels screw it up somehow.
>
> IBM and the personal computer business is a good example of that. I think as long as humans don't solve this human nature trait of sort of settling into a worldview after a while, there will always be opportunity for young companies, young people to innovate. As it should be.

It's Personal

One secret behind Steve's success is that his outreach was so profoundly personal. He knew how to connect with consumers in ways that made technology a part of humanity. His leadership style reflected his deep connection to what the interactions would be between product and user.

In an Apple store recently I overheard a conversation between a staff member and a customer about a technical issue, and what struck me was that the staffer was using the term *we*. Instead of talking about "the problem you're having," he was in effect saying, "We are all in the same boat here; let's work together to fix this problem."

Again the genius of Steve was reflected in the Apple store employees adopting the customer's viewpoint as part of the equation of solving problems: *us* instead of *you*. That's brilliant.

Steve and Students

Steve never forgot how his life had been turned around by a teacher who recognized he was a troublemaker in elementary school because he was so bright that he was bored, and through bribes and encouragement put him on a constructive path. Steve gave back what he had received from Mrs. Hill through a deep commitment to making computers available at significant discounts to schools, students, and faculty.

I once saw the effect firsthand. Steve and I were visiting an elementary school in Cupertino one day where the kids all had Apple computers. We were looking over their shoulders as they worked, noting with pleasure how they seemed to have mastered the machines and were able to work productively with them to speed their learning.

Late in the day, the teacher delivered us a note written by one of the kids. It read, "Mr. Jobs thank you for introducing me to the new Macintosh, I never ever thought I would be able to use a real computer in my life."

This was the kind of reward Steve needed to keep pursuing his art. For him, it was always personal, a quality I have found to be a major driver for anyone to become highly productive. He took the praise not for himself as a person but as what he was doing on behalf of that user, multiplied by every Apple user, everywhere.

Steve and Charitable Giving

Unlike almost any other major corporate executive you can name—with the exception in more recent years of American financier and businessman Warren Buffett and Microsoft's Bill Gates—Steve wasn't interested in the money. As far as we know, he never made any significant contributions to charity or to political campaigns, but he didn't spend very much, either—which in a way is curious, since he also once said that you don't want to leave your money to your children because it would ruin their lives.

But as a result, he has been sorely criticized for not establishing a charitable foundation like so many other mega-wealthy people.

Even back when he was still only a gigamillionaire, he and I talked about this a lot. He didn't believe in just giving money to some worthy but bureaucratic organizations that would take care of parceling out the funds, with no direct involvement of the donor.

He did feel that the way Apple donated and supported schools was a form of charitable giving, and one that had always been close to his heart. He had this feeling from his experience as a schoolchild and saw Apple's education program as a direct contribution to something he knew had a direct result.

Think of what Apple has done for education over the years: Billions of dollars in computers and software donated to school systems. Those steep price discounts. Computers donated to schools for development projects. A campaign that I helped him wage to obtain passage of what came to be known as "the Steve Jobs bill," which would have made donations of computer equipment to elementary school systems tax deductible—so that Apple and other corporations could donate even more generously.

To a lot of people, Steve's support of education doesn't count as charitable giving. Many thousands of teachers and school administrators would strongly disagree.

Legacy

As mentioned earlier, Steve's legacy was never more evident than at the 2012 Consumer Electronics Show (CES) in Las Vegas. His constantly beating the drum about the *user experience* had definitely caught hold: The phrase was a prominent feature of many product presentations. It was even true for Sony—a company that Steve had greatly admired from the early days, as well as having a two-way deep personal admiration for then-Sony CEO Akio Morita. The Sony booth at CES gave the impression that everyone must have gotten a memo about the importance of user experience as a term for catching customer interest. They were even handing out a press release, "Sony Delivers New User Experience for Consumers." And the president of Sony was being quoted as saying that the company had set up a user-experience organization dedicated to making sure all its products work well together. (Of course, Sony would be in much better shape today if they had listened to Steve touting the importance of user experience when he first started traveling to Japan and bringing it up in his conversations with Morita-san.)

Capturing the Steve Jobs Legacy

The concept of Apple University obviously stayed with Steve through the years. In 2008, he revived it, this time in a somewhat different form. He convinced Dr. Joel Podolny, the dean of Yale University's School of Management, to leave Yale and accept the title as dean of a revived Apple University. For some reason, Steve wanted to keep the project secret. Yale announced that Podolny was leaving to "lead educational initiatives at Apple"—clearly an intentionally cryptic phrase. Apple was silent, with not even a press release acknowledging Podolny's somewhat curious cover title as vice president of human resources, the same title I had once held.

Podolny had earlier been a faculty member at the Stanford Graduate School of Business, which is probably how Steve came to know of him. After becoming dean of Yale's management school, Podolny revamped the curriculum, replacing traditional courses in accounting and marketing with novel multidisciplinary programs. He was widely rumored to be in line for the position as a university president—a highly respected position and an opportunity it could not have been easy to walk away from. This was another example of the Jobsian powers of persuasion: when he decided on someone he wanted to hire, he was a very difficult man to say no to.

On leaving Yale, Podolny wrote to the students he was leaving behind, "While there are many great companies, I cannot think of one that has had a tremendous personal meaning for me as Apple." In fact, he had used an Apple II for doing writing assignments as far back as his undergraduate days at Harvard.

At Apple, a key part of his assignment was to explore the decision-making processes that had taken the company into some of its most unlikely directions, including the Apple stores and the iPhone. The lessons gleaned from examining these wildly successful deviations from the company's core business are now being taught to groups of up-and-coming Apple executives.

There was also a second task for Apple U, one even more significant for the training of future Apple managers. Podolny recruited other business school professors to help in the project of developing case studies. The goal: groom Apple executives in how to manage the Steve Jobs way. Steve had felt it vital to the company's future that Apple executives be taught to manage like him—since his management style was always such a contradiction from what is taught in traditional management courses. As part of this training, Steve identified the threads that he believed would sustain innovative leadership at Apple. His list included accountability, attention to detail, perfectionism, simplicity, and secrecy. The challenge would be to convey how these principles translate into business strategies and practices.

The case studies are intended to offer an understanding of what has made Apple and its products so successful. I'm told this involves digging through the Apple archives, talking to current and former employees and executives, seeking answers to the questions that define the decision-making process. Not on the technical side, of course, but on the management issues of how the company has chosen one project over another or selected whom to promote, trying to piece together Steve's reasons for firing people now and then, and the myriad other key choices in running what is arguably the most high-achieving company in history.

Of course, these case studies—no surprise here—are treated as top secret and are designed to be used for educating Apple's leaders and future leaders in thinking and decision-making.

As far as I've been able to learn, no other company has ever tried to capture and codify the thinking process of its leader or former leader. I can only hope that future historians and business executives will be allowed to pore through these case histories and share the wealth of wisdom they must contain. What fascinating reading that will be.

Developing innovative products and building nimble, creative organizations isn't what most people envision. It's not an easy life. Even if you have a great product, you have to protect and manage the environment surrounding every element, from development, through sales, to the upgrading or addition of a complementary product. It has to become a way of life—the essential ingredient if your hope is to walk in the footsteps of Steve.

New Man in Charge

In a much-quoted 2003 interview on the *60 Minutes* television program, Steve remarked, "Great things in business are almost never done by a single person." Yet the leadership of Apple was clearly dominated by one man. Now the reins have been passed, with Tim Cook doing what appears to be an eminently successful job of being the new Steve.

Clearly, the biggest challenge for Tim Cook as the new CEO of Apple is leading the company forward under that monumental shadow of Steve. Unlike some short-sighted leaders, Steve didn't surround himself with yes men who can't think for themselves. Instead, the team leaders he brought in to make Apple successful showed every sign of being completely capable of bearing the burdens that have been thrust upon them.

Perhaps the most brilliant part of Steve's legacy was finding Tim Cook and bringing him along year by year to be ready to step into the CEO's shoes whenever Steve needed to say goodbye to Apple. And perhaps that is the most important lesson in choosing your lieutenants: prepare someone who will be ready to take over for you, if and when.

The Apple Culture: Still in Place

Tim Cook had already, a couple of years earlier, reaffirmed his commitment to the business philosophy that Steve had expressed to me when he and I were fashioning Apple's first statement of values. Tim's words reflect how a strong corporate tradition and commitment can be passed along, embraced by the next generation of leadership. In an inspiring statement and affirmation, Tim said,

> There is an extraordinary depth and breadth and tenure among the Apple executive team, and these executives lead over 35,000 employees that I would call "all wicked smart." And that's in all areas of the company, from engineering to marketing to operations and sales and all the rest. And the values of our company are extremely well entrenched.
>
> We believe that we're on the face of the Earth to make great products, and that's not changing. We're constantly focusing on innovating. We believe in the simple, not the complex. We believe

that we need to own and control the primary technologies behind the products we make, and participate only in markets where we can make a significant contribution.

We believe in saying no to thousands of projects so that we can really focus on the few that are truly important and meaningful to us. We believe in deep collaboration and cross-pollination of our groups, which allow us to innovate in a way that others cannot.

And frankly, we don't settle for anything less than excellence in every group in the company, and we have the self-honesty to admit when we're wrong and the courage to change. And I think, regardless of who is in what job, those values are so embedded in this company that Apple will do extremely well.[1]

You can't help but admire any corporate leader who can express his commitment to excellence so effectively.

Tributes

Following the announcement of the death of Steve Jobs on October 5, 2011, Apple customers, Apple fans, and Steve Jobs admirers piled notes, flowers, and gifts outside Apple stores. This was a worldwide phenomenon that didn't happen for Walt Disney, Henry Ford, or Thomas Edison, and I believe may never happen again.

The day after Steve died, I was on a radio show on CNET for about three hours. During that time we received call after call from all over the world expressing sorrow at Steve's passing.

A couple of the calls really stood out in my mind. One was from Iran, from a person who had a smuggled a Mac into the country, obviously at great risk. Yet he could still say, "It's the best thing that ever happen to me."

The other most memorable call was from the bayous of Louisiana, from a crocodile hunter who said he was really sad.

The talk show host asked if he was a big Apple user.

"No," the man said.

"If you're not an Apple user," the host asked, "why are you sad?"

The man said, "Because I bought an iPhone and iPad for my children and they love the products and it is really helping in their education."

For me, those two calls epitomize the true contribution of Steve Jobs, the model and best example we may ever have of how a dynamic leader can change the world, one person at a time.

Finale

It only seemed fitting and in the Steve Jobs style that just after Steve's death, Apple's new CEO Tim Cook sent the following e-mail to all employees:

> Team,
>
> Like many of you, I have experienced the saddest days of my lifetime and shed many tears during the past week. But I've found some comfort in the extraordinary number of tributes and condolences from people all over the world who were touched by Steve and his genius. And I've found comfort in both telling and listening to stories about Steve.
>
> Although many of our hearts are still heavy, we are planning a celebration of his life for Apple employees to take time to remember the incredible things Steve achieved in his life and the many ways he made our world a better place. . . .
>
> I look forward to seeing you there.
>
> Tim

You can't connect the dots looking forward; you can only connect them looking backward. So you have to trust that the dots will somehow connect in your future. You have to trust in something—your gut, destiny, life, karma, whatever. This approach has never let me down, and it has made all the difference in my life. . . .

If you haven't found [your goal] yet, keep looking. Don't settle. As with all matters of the heart, you'll know when you find it. And, like any great relationship, it just gets better and better as the years roll on. . . .

The only way to be truly satisfied is to do what you believe is great work.

—Steve Jobs

Thank you, Steve, for connecting the dots by looking backward, while at the same time making the world a better place by always looking forward.

Notes

Chapter 1   A Ding in the Universe

1. Andy Reinhardt, "Steve Jobs: 'There's Sanity Returning,'" *BusinessWeek*, May 25, 1998.
2. Peter Burrows, "The Seed of Apple's Innovation," *BusinessWeek*, October 12, 2004.
3. Bill Taylor, "Decoding Steve Jobs: Trust the Art, Not the Artist," *Harvard Business Review Blog Network*, June 23, 2009.

Chapter 2   Steve's Business Philosophy and Values

1. From interview in William L. Simon and Jeffrey Young, *iCon* (Hoboken, NJ: John Wiley & Sons, 2005).
2. Tim Scannell, "Apple after Jobs," *Technology Guide*, undated.
3. Gary Wolf, "Steve Jobs: The Next Insanely Great Thing," *Wired*, April 2002, www.wired.com/wired/archive/4.02/jobs_pr.html.

Chapter 3   People Who Know More than You

1. John Markoff, "Apple and PC's, Both Given Up for Dead, Are Rising Anew," *New York Times*, April 26, 1999.

Chapter 4   Steve's Secrets for Selecting Great People

1. Rama Dev Jager and Rafael Ortiz, *In the Company of Giants: Candid Conversations with the Visionaries of the Digital World* (Darby, PA: Diane Pub Company, 1997).

2. David Ogilvy, *Confessions of an Advertising Man* (New York: Atheneum/Simon & Schuster, 1963), 47.
3. Tony Blair, *A Journey: My Political Life* (New York: Alfred A. Knopf, 2010), 9.
4. Jager and Ortiz, op. cit.
5. Sharlyn Lauby, "3 Ways to Find Top Talent for Your Startup," American Express OPEN Forum, September 24, 2011.

Chapter 5   Unusual Interviewing Techniques

1. Steve Jobs, "Steve Jobs Speaks Out," an interview with Senior Editor Betsy Morris, *Fortune*, August 3, 2008.
2. Eric Gelman et al, "Showdown in Silicon Valley," *Newsweek*, September 30, 1985, 47–50.

Chapter 6   To Protect Innovation, Create a Company within a Company

1. Rama Dev Jager and Rafael Ortiz, *In the Company of Giants: Candid Conversations with the Visionaries of the Digital World* (Darby, PA: Diane Pub Company, 1997).
2. "A Whiz Kid's Fall: How Apple Computer Dumped Its Chairman," *Newsweek*, September 30, 1985.

Chapter 7   "No More Crap Products"

1. Rob Walker, "The Guts of a New Machine," *New York Times*, November 30, 2003.
2. Walter Isaccson, *Steve Jobs* (Simon & Schuster, New York, 2011), p. 512
3. Ben Dobbin, "Kodak Engineer Had Revolutionary Idea: The First Digital Camera," September 8, 2005.

Chapter 8   More on Product Strategy

1. Ira Sager, Peter Burrows, and Andy Reinhardt, "Back to the Future at Apple," *BusinessWeek*, May 25, 1998.

Chapter 9   Entrepreneurial Confidence and High Standards

1. Steve Jobs, "Steve Jobs Speaks Out," an interview with Senior Editor Betsy Morris, *Fortune*, August 3, 2008.

Chapter 11   The Apple Workplace

1. Steve Jobs, "Steve Jobs Speaks Out," an interview with Senior Editor Betsy Morris, *Fortune*, August 3, 2008.

Chapter 12   When Selling Becomes More Important than the Product

1. Portfolio's Worst American CEOs of All Time, CNBC, undated; www.cnbc.com /id/30502091/Portfolio_s_Worst_American_CEOs_of_All_Time?slide=12.

Chapter 13   "And One More Thing"

1. Hugh Son, "Bank of America Backs Off from Plan to Charge Debit-Card Fee," *BusinessWeek*, November 2, 2011.
2. Bill Gates, "Content Is King," Microsoft.com, January 3, 1996, http://web .archive.org/web/20010126005200/http://www.microsoft.com/billgates/columns /1996essay/essay960103.asp.
3. Michael Helft, "Steve Jobs' Real Legacy: Apple Inc.," *Fortune*, September 8, 2011.

Chapter 14   Flowers at His Doorstep

1. Tim Cook, "Apple Inc. F1Q09 (Qtr End 12/27/08) Earnings Call Transcript," *Seeking Alpha*, January 21, 2009, http://seekingalpha.com/article/115797-apple -inc-f1q09-qtr-end-12-27-08-earnings-call-transcript.
2. The boxed quote is from the Steve Jobs speech to the graduating class at the Stanford University commencement, June 2005. Copyright Stanford University, 2005. The entire remarkable speech can be read or viewed at many places on the Internet.

Acknowledgments

It would be difficult to fully express my appreciation to Bill Simon for his efforts. Working with Bill on a book is like working with Steve Jobs on the development of a product. As Steve always had the user in mind, Bill always has the reader in mind: "Jay, will the reader really get this?" or "I'm not sure there is a lesson here for the reader." It's because of this passion for the reader that these books have been so great. Bill, as Steve Jobs would say, "you are insanely great," and you are a wonderful writer. Thanks for your remarkable support.

The other part of the puzzle is having great publishers. Richard Narramore of John Wiley & Sons, Inc. proved to be a demanding, insightful, and inspiring editor, and I'm grateful for his guidance.

I would like to recognize Hoepli Editore in Milan for setting the standard, when they published my previous book in Italy. I realize this success was in part due to the brilliant title that Hoepli selected: *Steve Jobs: The Man Who Invented the Future*. Not only did the book become the number-one best seller, but it totally beat all expectations for copies sold, which led the esteemed Ulrico Hoepli to ask for this follow-up. So a special thanks to Ulrico and to the rest of Hoepli team who have worked on these books: Barbara Hoepli, Andrea Sparacino, and Maurizio Vedovati. I especially appreciate Barbara Hoepli's great marketing plan and her warm hospitality on my trips to Italy.

A true tribute to the Hoepli effort is the thousands of letters, e-mails, and calls I have received from readers in Italy, as well as others from all over the world. Many of these readers indicated that *The Steve Jobs Way* had changed the way they were going to approach their business. I particularly want to acknowledge two readers of my previous book, who helped me shape the information presented here: Fred Marshall, CEO of Quantum Learning, Inc., who clearly understood the lessons needed for future organizations and how to apply them to a company's ecosystem, and Matthew Moore of CrowdMob, Inc., who epitomizes the reader seeking information about Steve Jobs that he could apply to his business. After reading my book, Matt had me address his employees to help shape the future of his business. It is this kind of response that really recognizes the influence Steve's way had on our world.

I would be remiss if I did not acknowledge the support and advice from my literary agent, Bill Gladstone. Bill, as usual, played a major role in getting this book project developed. And my many thanks for getting the other Bill involved again. Without the both of you, this project would not have happened.

Index